Journey into Love

Ten Steps to Wholeness

Kani Comstock & Marisa Thame

WILLOW PRESS

Published by Willow Press
241 Village Park Drive
Ashland, OR 97520

Cover Photo by Jim Chadwick
Cover and Interior Design by Lightbourne

Publisher's Cataloging-in-Publication
(Provided by Quality Books, Inc.)

Comstock, Kani.
    Journey into love : ten steps to wholeness /
Kani Comstock and Marisa Thame. -- 1st ed.
    p. cm.
    ISBN: 0-9679186-4-2

    1. Love. 2. Self-actualization (Psychology)
3. Spirituality. I. Thame, Marisa. II. Title.

BF575.L8C66 2000   158.2
           QBI00-900195

Printed in the United States of America
10 9 8 7 6 5 4 3

To our parents, who gave us life
and taught us more than we will ever know.

And to Bob Hoffman, whose work reconnected us with our essence,
and enabled us to love ourself, our parents and others
for who we all really are.

Contents

Acknowledgments

W riting this book is the culmination of many years of working with the Hoffman Quadrinity Process® as students of the Process and of the creator, Bob Hoffman, as Process teachers, and as trainers of Process teachers.

We give our heartfelt appreciation and love to Bob Hoffman for all the knowledge and richness this journey has brought into our lives.

We thank all our many students who have given us the honor of being of service to them and of learning from each of them.

We thank our fellow teachers, with whom we have shared many experiences and discussions and from whom we have learned many things, for their support for the writing of this book.

We thank every Quadrinity Process teacher in the world for their commitment to creating peace within their students and through them creating more peace in the world.

We thank our friends for supporting us and encouraging us in writing this book, and giving us nurturance when we needed it.

We thank Barbara Comstock for her careful reading, in-depth discussions, insightful suggestions, and unending support.

You all have our love and gratitude.

And we thank each other for our vision, dedication, and discipline, and the respect, admiration, and love we feel for each other.

Both of us have found fulfillment in personally experiencing the journey we describe in this book. It changed our lives and continues to unfold. In the years since that experience, we each have dedicated our self to deepening our understanding of this journey and sharing it with others. Our knowledge comes from our personal experience of the journey as students and as teachers of thousands of students, and from our training and work directly with the creator, Bob Hoffman, who died in 1997. While the theory, concepts, and techniques are clearly his, we take full responsibility for our interpretation and description.

This book is not about the particulars of our journey. Rather the subject is the challenge of freeing ourselves from false limitations and controlling images and being who we truly are—a challenge that can be addressed in various ways.

Introduction

I was an achiever. I had a good life—an executive position, challenging work which brought me satisfaction, and a loving relationship. I looked like a success.

Actually I was a workaholic driven to always do more, who didn't know how to play and couldn't achieve balance in my life. I was in a relationship with an angry man just as driven as I was, who directed his considerable hostility at me when he wasn't his usual charming, creative, productive self. After decades of total suppression, the anger I didn't know existed in me was erupting in baffling ways. I'd tried for many years in many ways to change things, but I always came back to a similar, familiar place.

I wanted more fullness in my life—more joy, playfulness, peace—but I didn't know how to achieve it. After my last concerted attempt to change had failed, I felt hopeless and resigned. I was certain that the most I could expect in life was to work long hours toward an ever expanding goal, then collapse in exhaustion on some lovely beach until I caught my breath and could start all over again.

Then I was faced with an opportunity to travel the path described in this book. Learning about this journey into love triggered deep skepticism. I was certain I didn't have a problem with love. The only two problems I had were that I didn't know how to play, and that I had this alien anger in my gut. But the concepts, which this book explains, made sense.

In many ways I had idealized my childhood. I thought my mother and father had been better than most parents, that they had been loving and supportive. In looking back at my childhood to identify some negativity, I remembered that

I had loved gymnastics and had always wanted to learn ballet. When I begged to take lessons, I was told that I was clumsy and lessons would be a waste of hard-earned money. That small memory ripped at my heart, and seemingly endless tears came unbidden. I realized that despite the decades that had passed, I still carried the hurt fresh and strong as it had been then. I recognized that even though I have always been agile and graceful, I viewed myself as clumsy, and had disowned the body I live in. That was the opening connection I made between painful childhood experiences and limitations in my adult life.

Over time I came to recognize many others much larger. I realized that in my family, achievement was the only route to attention and acceptance; it was never enough to *be*. I saw that the frightening anger that, at moments, possessed my being was hauntingly like my explosive father who I swore I would never be like, and yet adored when he was not angry. I realized that I was a victim of my partner's rage just as my mother had been, and became oblivious to my fear when his good humor returned.

I experienced the battle within myself between hope—that this work could shift my life into balance and richness, and skepticism—that change is difficult and slow if it happens at all, and certainly doesn't last. And amazingly I listened to the small, compelling voice that urged me to "go for it."

It wasn't until after I (Kani) started the journey described in this book that I experienced how much I needed love, how great my alienation was from my own spirit, how similar I was to my parents in their dysfunction. The journey into love challenged me to be authentic. It changed my life. It brought me what I was looking for, and more than I knew was possible. It opened me to the abundance of choices available to me, expanding the dimensions of my life. It was an epic journey. Now I can barely grasp what life was like before.

In myths, a hero is often faced with a series of challenges. To gain the prize, he or she must understand what is necessary, figure out a strategy for accomplishing the task, find the courage, and do what is necessary. Each challenge prepares the hero for, and leads directly into, the next.

One prize we all desire, whether we recognize it or not, is love. We need love that will validate our being, that will nurture us unconditionally. A limitless source of love awaits us within. It is our essence, our spirit, our core. But our access to it has been blocked, the flow disrupted. We have lost sight of its presence. The resulting drought has distorted our life. Often we don't know what we thirst for. We have taken on characteristics of who we are not.

The "journey into love" has ten distinct challenges, ten steps which must be accomplished in sequence. Success at addressing each challenge opens the gateway to the next. This book identifies the ten steps, locates the gates along the path, explains why each step is necessary, and describes what we can experience as we accomplish them one by one. Like any guidebook, *Journey Into Love* does not replace the travel—it prepares us to make the trip. It describes destinations we barely knew existed and makes them accessible. It provides a map and gives us hope that we can successfully make the journey. The book stays focused on what needs to be accomplished to reach our goal.

This is a powerful spiritual journey to wholeness and love which culminates in integration. It brings authenticity. It connects us to our inner wisdom, frees our creativity, and opens us to possibilities we had no idea existed.

I

Moving
into
Awareness

*The journey into love begins with
understanding how we lost sight of our
essence, our spirit, our source of love. In order
to survive in childhood, we took on a false self
comprised of compulsive patterns which are
not us, but define, control and limit us.
Awareness that these patterns are not us,
brings us hope that we can change.*

I magine, if you can, that we were each conceived as positive joyous unique beings full of love and curiosity, and eager to enter the world. And the woman and man who gave us life—our parents—want to do everything they can to love us and make our life better than theirs has been. They care for us in the best way they know how, providing for us everything that they can.

But our parents are not us, and they cannot conceive of everything we want or need. They cannot even perceive all of what their own needs are. And in trying to care for us as well as themselves and each other, their attention is of necessity divided. At times their needs take precedent over ours, and in fulfilling those needs they may ignore us, abandon us, or even inflict harm on us indirectly or directly. They may be so self-absorbed that they can only see us as a reflection of themselves or a barrier to their happiness. Or worse, our parents never wanted us, perhaps they didn't even love each other, and they feel burdened by our existence and overwhelmed by the demands on them.

As infants and small children we need a continuous, uninterrupted flow of unconditional acceptance and love to validate our existence. Our parents are the center of our universe. We're dependent on them to meet all of our physical and emotional needs. We need to see our being reflected back as loved and accepted to feel connected and safe. At the moments when the flow of love is diverted, we panic. We feel unlovable and abandoned. We cannot blame the parent, who seems all knowing, all powerful. We can only blame our self and assume that we are not good enough, that we are somehow flawed, defective.

Earning love

Our basic strategy for *earning* love is imitating the people we so desperately need love from—our parents. We assume that if we become *like* the parent, then he or she will accept and love us. Whenever we feel unlovable, we try to earn parental love. This occurs on an emotional and physical level long before our intellect is active; it starts in the womb and continues to puberty. It happens especially when our parents are distracted or absent or when they are giving us negative attention because they do not like the way we are behaving.

We act out mother's or father's behavior as we perceive it, mirroring it back to our parent, and in doing so are in effect saying, "Look at me, I'm just like you. Now will you love me?" And sometimes they *do* love us then and we feel accepted once again. In effect, we *learn* that we can earn love this way. At other times, our parent doesn't notice us at all, or becomes angry, resenting our innocent attempts to mirror their negative behaviors. Then we try even harder to be like them. In this way we take on our parents' negative behaviors, moods, attitudes, and beliefs as well as their positive ones and act them out automatically, unconsciously, and compulsively over and over again. Even seemingly positive behaviors are negative when they are imitation and driven rather than authentic.

Learning to imitate our parents' patterns—their behaviors, moods, attitudes and beliefs—rather than listening to our inner wisdom, we lose touch with who we really are. We learn to deny our essential being and come to believe that their traits define who we are. We want to be loved for who we are, but we learn to elicit love by acting like our parents who we fear might, otherwise, reject and abandon us.

Here is our predicament: we need our parents' love, yet

resent their failure to see us and love us for who we really are. Resentment arouses an impulse to hurt them as we have been hurt. We discover that by imitating their negative traits, we can get back at our parents in a seemingly safe way—by being like them. We take the behaviors that we adopted from them to earn their love and use these behaviors against them. We learn how to make our parents wince by experiencing how they make us wince. We have all observed children do this, even if we cannot remember doing it ourselves. This getting back at our parents is the underside of the need for love that created the behavior in the beginning.

Any absence of love is experienced as emotional abandonment, and the ultimate loss is physical abandonment, as when a parent leaves or dies. If we lose one or both of our parents very early in life, even if we're adopted very shortly thereafter, we experience and suffer the consequences of this abandonment. The separation from our biological parent creates the first sensation in us that we are not valued, that we are not good enough. Unconsciously we suffer the fear of further abandonment, even from surrogate parents who are actually loving us and caring for us. We feel resentful and vindictive toward those who abandoned us and also those who, we fear, might abandon us in the future.

Ways of adopting patterns

There are four ways we adopt patterns from our parents. For example, our parents are critical. We can be self-critical, always judging ourselves and finding fault and putting ourselves down. Or we can be critical of others. Or we can be attracted to people who are critical of us just as our parents were and then act in ways that invite criticism from them. Or we can be attracted to people who are critical of others, and act in ways to encourage their criticism. In other words, (1) we can do it to ourselves; (2) we can do it to others; (3) we can set it up for others to act towards us just as our parents did; or (4) we can encourage people to act critically towards others just as our parents did. In the first and second case it is we who are being critical; in the first and third, it is we who are the target; and in the fourth case we are neither the target or attacker, rather we are an observer of others being critical and criticized.

	Target	
	self	*other*
self	1	2
Critic		
other	3	4

For many of our adopted patterns we may do all four.

This is straight adoption of parental traits. Many of the behaviors, moods and attitudes that we adopt are never put into words. Even in the womb we start adopting moods simply as a result of the chemicals created in our mother's body as she experiences various moods.

If our mother smiles whenever others are present, she teaches us that only positive feelings are acceptable in the presence of others. Like her we learn to deny and repress the other feelings we have and smile compulsively. If our father is always busy and takes no time to play with us, we learn that we are not worthy of attention and that only achievement is valued.

Rebellion

Now the process gets more tricky. As we gain experience of life, we notice that some of the behaviors of our parents feel terrible. We know we don't want to be like them, at least in those ways. So we rebel and say "No" to that behavior. We make a point of rejecting their pattern and acting out a different one. This feels powerful, it feels like choice. But in rebellion we are still acting compulsively. Our compulsion has now become to appear different, just as earlier we sought to be the same.

What starts out as a decision to rebel, quickly becomes unconscious, automatic and compulsive. We act differently than our parents in order to reject them, get back at them, be better than them. The trouble is we still crave their love and acceptance. The conflict is inescapable. The better we do as a rebel, the more we risk being rejected. Even though we rebel, our repressed adoption of the pattern lives in us too and we are torn. So rebellion is just as unsatisfactory as adoption.

The Negative Love Syndrome— internalizing our parents

We want our parents' love so we adopt all of their patterns in the process of trying to earn that love, and we rebel. Bob Hoffman names this the Negative Love Syndrome. By trying to earn love, we become inauthentic, an imitation. This falseness is negative, therefore the name negative love. The end result of negative love is that we always get what we most fear, the opposite of what we want. We want to be loved and we end up feeling unlovable. We fear rejection and abandonment and we set it up to be rejected. And we can't see that we are not what we appear to be. We have lost touch with our inner truth and strength.

When both parents are very much the same, the programming is very deep and often invisible to us because it appears that is the way life is—it's natural, everyone feels that way or does it that way. There is no other choice except to rebel. When each parent is different, then we have a dilemma. To earn each of their love, we must adopt opposing patterns, which creates conflict. When we are acting out mother's pattern, then we are in rebellion to father. When we are acting out father's behavior, we are in rebellion to mother. There is no comfortable course, we are in conflict, but at least we know that two options exist.

As our intellect's analytical abilities develop, it is faced with the monumental task of making sense out of the adopted negative patterns and the rebellions and the apparent need to defend them. In fact we have become our parents even while appearing different from them. We have internalized our parents, we have unconsciously taken them into our being. They whisper in our ears and send thoughts whirling around our minds. They control our lives regardless of how far we physically move away from them. They live on in us even if they are dead.

We see the world through our parents' eyes and hear with their ears. Often we hear ourselves speaking with their voice, using their words, feeling their feelings, and experience our bodies moving as their body does. At these moments we are in touch with how we have become our parents and how automatic these moments are. For the rebels among us, these are especially humbling occurrences.

Transferring our parents onto others

We go through life relating to others as if they are our parents. We've all felt that negative reaction to another that's quickly followed by the feeling or belief that we know what they are thinking, what their intentions are and what all of their faults are. We are certain we know what is going on with them. Sometimes this happens before they've even spoken or after only a few words. Sometimes it happens after a relationship has been established. We react to them from the belief that we know everything about them because in some part of us, we have been triggered to believe they are just like our parent—and we know what to expect from mom and dad. This automatic reaction to someone is called *transference.* Transference takes us out of the present moment and back to being a child again. We feel our loss of power and the need to protect our self. It brings us back to our childhood survival strategies. Transference deprives us of the opportunity to know what is actually going on in the present. We have lost our curiosity about who the other person really is, what they are actually thinking and what they are feeling. When we are in transference, in fact, there is only our self and our parent. No one else exists. And we are usually oblivious to what has happened.

Often we perceive one behavior and automatically extrapolate to a perceived in-depth understanding of the other person—suddenly we feel we know all about them. And we feel all the anger at others that we felt at our parents for not experiencing us for who we are. Many of us have felt that every boss we've had is just like our father (or maybe mother depending on who the authority was in our family). We experience our lovers like our parents—"He's stubborn, therefore angry and vindictive just like my father!" or "She's withholding, therefore unaffectionate and blaming just like both my parents." Transference deprives us of knowing who the other person really is and of experiencing real relationship with another.

Negative programming is a powerful force. When we adopt the negative behaviors, moods, attitudes and beliefs of either or both parents into our being, we are relating to them in Negative Love. In our childhood it was a reactive strategy for survival. As adults it keeps us stuck in the pain of our childhood, repeating endlessly the same patterns that made us feel unlovable then.

What is love?

There are so many understandings of love. Each of us called what we received in our childhood love even if the word was never used. We needed love and we found a way to label what we received as love. Some of us had parents who seemed loving, saying the right words, doing the right things, but we couldn't feel the love. They were trying to love, but no one taught them about love so they couldn't give it to us and we felt we were at fault. Some of us had needy parents who tried to earn love from us by giving us attention or things— giving because they needed love from us. Others of us had parents who were overprotective, so afraid some harm would come to us, or guilty because they hadn't really wanted us and consequently needed to appear to be the perfect parent. Some of us had parents who did everything that was required of them to fulfill their duty as parents, but without feeling. Some of us had parents who always made everything pleasant and couldn't acknowledge or validate our full range of feelings. Some of us had parents who were determined that we have everything that they didn't have in their life so that they could live vicariously through us. Others of us had parents who were emotionally unpredictable, moving between safety and abuse without warning, keeping us for-ever on our toes and slightly off balance. Some of us had parents who said in effect, "I'll love you if you're good!" Others of us had parents who set no restrictions or bound-aries at all; they let us do whatever we wanted without reaction. We each called it love and said to ourselves, "My parents love me."

If these actions aren't love, then what is love? We could say that love is the outpouring of emotional goodness *to our self first*, and then to others in our lives. Love cannot be given if it is not felt first for our self. We cannot receive love from others to fill our selves.

In order to understand how our programming affects our being, let's consider that each of us has four aspects of self, which are interactive. These aspects are our physical body, our intellect, our emotions and our spirit.

Our spirit

Our essence is the totally positive, joyous, unique aspect of self which is full of love. This is the non-physical aspect most present when we are conceived. It is knowing, wise, loving and powerful. It knows and strives for truth and jus-tice, aspires to goodness, is completely ethical and has total integrity. It is the part of us that is self-reflective and can observe us impartially. It's the source of our intuition, spon-taneity and creativity. It's grounded and centered. It is our connection to the universe and to the divine. It is our spirit.

We came into the world fully in touch with this aspect of our self and were not seen by our parents for who we were. Instead we were driven to take on their patterns and become other than what we are. And in the process we lost touch with our essence, our spirit; in fact, we were programmed to deny it. Some of us remember moments of connection with this vital life force within and ardently strive to return to that experience. Others of us have lost the memories and belief in our essence to such an extent that we deny that it even exists. But we all experience it at moments throughout our life.

There are times in nature when we feel at peace and at one with the universe. Or in the midst of trauma and chaos, suddenly we feel calm and know that everything will be all right. These are the moments when our spirit has pierced through our defensive armor of denial to fill us with its peace, wisdom and love, and we feel blessed.

Our emotions

Our emotional self is the aspect of relatedness and connection. It moves us outside our self to connect with others. This aspect awakens fully in our infancy and reflects our experience in feelings which span a wide range in kind and intensity. As infants we move through experiences from one to the other with curiosity, and our feelings move just as quickly. Initially we have no inhibitions. All feelings are acceptable whether we are laughing, content, happy, scared, sad or crying. We are not attached to any of them, they are all equal. They are all expressions of our being. They provide us with information about what is going on within us and help us orient our self in the world.

Judgments enter our feeling world—we get the message from our parents that what we are feeling and expressing is not acceptable, and we don't know why. But we learn quickly to follow their lead and mirror their behaviors back to them so we can feel the acceptance and love we yearn for, that complete our need for connection with them. We take on all their feelings, and become like them with their fear, guilt, anxiety, defensiveness, unworthiness, inadequacy and denial. We become who we are not in order to survive.

Our emotional self was not validated for who it was in childhood and thus its development is arrested. It remains an emotional child within, carrying all the pain, the guilt, the humiliation, the shame and the anger of a lifetime. Our emotional child learned its own specific strategy for survival from our experiences with our particular parents. Each of us has our own unique complex of patterns. These patterns are not the source of our problems, they are reflections of a deeper wound—that we did not feel loved. As a result, today we feel unlovable and alienated from our true feelings.

Our intellect

Our intellect is the aspect of thought, perception and reflection. Our intellect starts to awaken in our early school years, but is not fully active until many years later. It is rational, analytical and conceptual. It grasps new information, evaluates, synthesizes and integrates it into our existing knowledge, and then organizes and expresses ideas. It strives to make "sense" out of our feelings and experiences, and the world. It seeks truth and awareness.

From the beginning our intellect is faced with the monumental task of trying to decipher meaning in the already well-developed negative patterns which control our early life. Our intellect is programmed through our emotional child to defend the parental programming which started before the intellect was fully active. Our intellect is forced to focus its considerable talents and energy on rationalizing and justifying everything it learns from our emotional child and from our parents about who we are. Our intellect believes that it's defending our being, while in reality it's defending patterns learned from our parents and is already in denial of who we really are. Its abilities are being limited. Instead of an open, eager, curious mind, there is judgment, criticism and rigidity. And no matter how hard we try, we cannot make sense of it all. We experience so many contradictory thoughts and beliefs: I'm stupid or know it all, superior or inferior, special or worthless. We yearn for order and understanding and try to control our world to make it fit our needs.

Emotional child and intellect interactions

Our emotional child looks to our emerging intellect for the validation it doesn't receive from our parents. And our developing intellect looks to the emotional child for the sense of meaning that it craves. Neither our child nor our intellect finds what they want in the other. So they each blame the other just as they have been blamed by our parents for not being what they should be. We experience the battle between our child and intellect as an internal dialogue, as chatter in the head—those voices that whisper or shout the messages that grab our attention away from the moment, away from the present and back into the past. These are the voices of our parents in us played out by our child and intellect as if they were us. They use all the parental patterns they have learned against each other in a desperate attempt to be all right. And when that doesn't work, then they collude with one another.

Addictions are prime examples of this collusion. The child needs relief from its feelings of unlovability; it needs to feel connected and loved and so it turns to a substance or behavior which represses its unlovable feeling and creates the illusion of being loved and connected. And the intellect, needing relief from its constant search for order, rationalizes the choice and says, "Yes, this is a good idea." It could be food, alcohol, drugs, exercise, sex, romance, gambling, work, risk, adrenaline. And for a little time we feel good, but that dissipates and we're faced with the consequences. Our disappointed and disillusioned intellect turns to our child and blames it again in order to escape any responsibility for the action. And the war moves on.

Our body

Our physical body is the aspect present when we are conceived. It is the carrier of genetic information and the repository for the memories of all our experiences. It provides physical expression to our emotions, intellect and spirit and is the "house," the physical dwelling for these three non-physical aspects: the mind. Our body is interconnected with our non-physical mind through neurological and biochemical feedback systems. It provides us with sensation and mobility.

In the beginning of our existence our body was at one with our spirit. As our emotions and intellect develop and conflicts arise, our body manifests the patterns and the conflicts. Our body experiences the stress, anxiety and depression, the food disorders, the psychosomatic pains and illnesses, the various addictions, the self-destruction.

Our body expresses the programs of our emotional child and our intellect and it takes on patterns of its own directly from our parents. How many of us have been told that we walk just like our father or smile like our mother? There is also the shame of our body, the feeling that it's too fat or thin or all wrong, the coldness and lack of affection, the inability to enjoy sex. The patterns that we adopt from our parents even change our body chemistry.

Interaction between the four aspects

These four aspects are not separate and distinct. They are interacting all the time. This is a simple model for a complex system, but it helps us to grasp the dynamics of what is occurring within us so we can find some understanding and resolution of the dissonance in our life.

In negative love, the four aspects of self—our quadrinity—are alienated and in conflict. We experience dis-harmony, dis-integration and dis-connection. We find our choice of being like our parents, or rebelling against them, limited and unsatisfying. We want there to be something better than what we have.

Our quadrinity in adulthood

As adults we have within us an emotional child, often called our *inner child.* This child of ours carries the pain from our childhood which keeps it imprisoned as a hurt child with no sense of time or space. We can be triggered over and over again by some small event in our adult life and suddenly we find our self back in childhood, feeling those same feelings just as intensely as when we were actually there. And we want to strike back or escape or shut down just as we did as a child.

It's so easy for most of us to get stuck in the negative feelings and minimize or avoid the positive. Many of us scan regularly for the negative, skipping right over anything that is in good shape or going well, and focus all of our attention on what is wrong or lacking, just as we learned to do from our parents. The Pollyannas among us have learned just the opposite—to scan for the positive and repress or deny the rest, a behavior which is often the result of and the perfect setup for repeated abuse.

Our programmed adult intellect is often oblivious to the existence of our little emotional child. The intellect values only logic and thought and since it cannot trust others, it believes that it alone carries the burden of finding the solution to life's problems. The arrogance of our intellect is that it often thinks it is our spirit or, if not that, then that it is the only way to our spirit. Our intellect often runs our life trying to make sense out of non-sense and disowning the non-logical. Its programming limits its vision. Myopically and compulsively our intellect repeats its patterns, thus denying its true limitations and strengths.

Our adult body has been paying the price since childhood. As the years progress, its defenses often diminish and more and more physical symptoms appear. We all have some. For many of us it's headaches and back pain. For some it's frequent illness—colds and flu—or chronic illnesses such as ulcers, colitis, high blood pressure, fibromyalgia, chronic fatigue syndrome, cancer, heart disease. The research is demonstrating more and more connections between the mind and the body. There are numerous bestsellers on this subject. Many of us have learned to ignore the symptoms, to deny their validity and importance. We treat our body as if it is separate from our mind instead of reflective of it.

And of our spirit there are only flashes, precious moments of inner peace and love. What once filled our being is now hidden from us under layers of negative programming that makes us feel we are something other than our true essence. When we ask ourselves "who am I?" or "what do I want in life?" we are searching for this aspect. It is the part of us that brings us to growth and learning, that strives for unity and integration, that brings us serenity, that is wise and fills us with love.

Hope for a better future

Understanding the Negative Love Syndrome brings us hope that we are not who we think we are, we are not all the hundreds of patterns we learned in order to survive our childhood. In fact, the hope is that we are much better than we can imagine. Recognizing that we have learned the negative patterns, that they are not us, brings us hope that we can change, that we can become who we really are.

2

Committing
to
Change

*Our desire to change our self and our life
arises from our dissatisfaction with what is,
regardless of how successful and fulfilled our
life appears to be. Hope that change is possible,
along with recognition of the specifics of what's
wrong with our life, moves us to commit to
change. Commitment energizes the change
process and enables it to flow.*

Change is personal and specific. Our desire to change our self or our life comes out of a dissatisfaction with specifics of our present situation, regardless of how good that is. We want certain things to be different. Without hope that lasting change is possible, we feel resigned to endure what is.

Change shakes up our *status quo*. We may not like the way things are now, but it is familiar, we know what to expect and we feel we can manage it. Change is a risk. Change means walking into the unknown, the unfamiliar. Change is often uncomfortable. It means doing something we don't know how to do—if we did, we would have already done it. We often feel cautious and tentative doing something for the first time, uncertain whether we are doing it right. One fear is that change will be worse than what we have now. Another fear is that after all the effort and raised expectations, nothing will really change at all—it will all return to the way it is now.

For many of us, unless we hit a crisis, we avoid looking at what's wrong with our life. Or we look only at the surface. Otherwise it feels too depressing. We may feel that we cannot fix all that is wrong item by item, so we look for a magical solution, the one thing that when changed will shift the whole situation. It might be a new relationship or getting married or having a baby or a new job or a raise or winning the lottery or a vacation or falling in love or moving to a new house or new city, perhaps a new country or getting stoned or getting sober. And we work for that one thing and we expect our whole life to be better. And it's better perhaps, but still not satisfying.

Often we live on the surface of life because it feels too painful when we delve deeper. We don't know what to do with the pain, the hurt, the shame, the anger, the resentments, the depression, the imbalances, the emptiness, the loneliness, the feelings of unlovability. We stick with what we know, it feels safe. And it has the comfort of familiarity even if it's unsatisfactory. We know we can survive just as we always have—we've been doing it since childhood.

At some point in our life, however, we stop and say, "There has to be more." We know on some level, regardless of all we've achieved inwardly and outwardly in our life, that now we're ready to make the journey back to our self, to our essence, to our wholeness. We are finally willing to determine what it is we really want and to ask for it. We are ready to know who we really are, to feel love and acceptance for our self, and to live from that love in the world.

We, the authors, have personally traveled this journey and have also assisted thousands of other people on the journey back to themselves and to their abundant love within. Regardless of how terrible any of us feel we are or appear to be, each one of us does have a totally positive, powerful and loving essence. In all our experience with this work we've never found even one person with a negative or evil core. Certainly we all have many negative patterns, but our essence, our spirit, is wondrously whole, powerful, wise and loving.

Looking at our life with curiosity

We need to look at our life with a critical eye and identify what is wrong with our current life—everything that's amiss in all areas of our life. Many of us already have long lists in our minds. There may be an urge to stop after identifying one major flaw and believe that if this is one thing is corrected, our life will be transformed. We often must force ourselves to persist in exploring beyond the most obvious, to see the compromises we have made, the ways in which we have submitted, complied and given up our dreams, the beliefs we hold about our self and the world, our willingness to settle for what it appears we can have. We need to be curious about how we have delineated the limits of our life. Often the opening revelation is one little thing that we have overlooked or pushed aside as insignificant. Seeing just one aspect of our life from a new perspective often encourages us to delve into our search with curiosity.

Pattern tracing

Having identified patterns, then we can look for the connection between what is wrong in our life now and how we learned to be that way in our childhood from our parents. In doing this we also need to notice where we rebelled against our parents and chose an alternative compulsion. This is *pattern tracing*—identifying the negative pattern in our current life and tracing it back to our childhood and noticing how we learned it and who we learned it from. Was it mother or father or both, or possibly a surrogate parent? Surrogate parents include any parental figure who was not our biological parent, but was a parental figure in our childhood, and may include adoptive parents, step-parents, grandparents or a nanny, for example. Our programming resulted from our relationship with each and every parent from conception to puberty. If we were adopted at birth and never even "knew" our biological parents, we are still programmed by them.

It is important to recognize that behaviors, moods, attitudes and beliefs are not of themselves positive or negative.

When they are automatic, compulsive, unconscious, then they are programming from our childhood and we refer to them as negative love patterns. Think of behaviors like workaholism or compulsive honesty or over-responsibility or caretaking, for example. When we are freed from the compulsion of these patterns, then we can choose to use the skill for our benefit and it's no longer negative.

Our relationship with our inner self

What kind of relationship do we have with our inner emotional child? How old is our inner child? Do we even recognize its existence? And if we do, how often can we listen to it, validate it and nurture it? What are its fears, its needs? How often is its voice silent and afraid? Or does it run the show? How do we relate to our adult intellect? Do we trust it, value it? Is it always in charge, self-centered, the know-it-all, the voice of authority, judgment and criticism? Or is it confused, inadequate or lonely? What kind of relationship do we have with our spirit? Have we learned to deny or doubt its existence? Do we deny our spirituality, negate the existence of a higher power? Do we believe that God is outside of us, that we have to be good to be loved by God? Do we turn to God only when we want something or have guilt and fear?

How we feel about our body

When we look at our body in the mirror, do we feel, "This is a wonderful body I have?" Can we marvel in the beauty of its movement and sensation, its sensuality? Do we feel really present and connected with our body? Or do we notice only the things we don't like? Are we ashamed of it? Is it the wrong size or shape? Do we nurture and care for our body, giving it healthful food, exercise, rest and sleep? Or do we abuse it or use it carelessly or ignore it? How do we feel about our gender? Are we proud of it and love being what we are? Do we accept our sexuality and our sexual orientation? Do we feel free to think about sex, to talk about it, and to express our sexuality and sensuality? Is sex integrated into our life or in a space apart, secret, dangerous and dirty?

Making the connections

With the awareness of how we relate to our different aspects (emotions, intellect, spirit and body) we can go back into memories of our childhood and notice how our parents related to themselves, and how they related to those aspects of us. Maybe they behaved a certain way only once, but we learned it. We need to notice from whom we learned each pattern: mother, father or surrogate parents. We need to see those connections because in seeing the specific connections, the reality of negative love grows in us and builds our determination to be free.

Our relationship with our parents as adults

Do we love spending time with our parents as adults and enjoy sharing our thoughts and feelings with them? Do we enjoy doing many things together? Or is our tolerance limited to a few minutes or hours at a time, planned activities and superficial talk? Do we find ourselves feeling like children around them even when we have children of our own? Do we feel controlled or manipulated by them? Do they act to make us feel guilty that we don't spend more time with them? Do we live so far away from them that we rarely have to see them at all? Or do we hate to be with them and don't want to stay together more than a few minutes? Do we have an illusion about the quality of our adult relationship with our parents, thinking it is much better than it really is? Do we treat our parents now just like they treated us as children, and now we are the authority and they are dependent?

Our relationship to siblings, colleagues and friends

Siblings are the people closest to us in the world biologically, physiologically and in experience, even more than our mother and father. Do we have close, loving, nurturing relationships with all of them, with any of them? Do we trust them and turn to them for advice and sharing? Can we share our secrets with them? Are our siblings our only real friends—it's us against the world? Are we superficial friends? Are we in competition with them, always comparing our self to them and seeing who's ahead? Do we keep our distance from them, afraid of being hurt? Are we holding resentments? Do we ignore them and think that we have no problem because we never felt that our relationship had any importance?

How we learned to relate to our siblings affects how we come to relate to friends and co-workers. What are those relationships like? Are they just like our relationships with our siblings or have we rebelled? Do we have close friends? Many or just a few? Are they friends we share our deepest thoughts and feelings with or only share activities with? Do our relationships endure? Are we always taking care of others or are we a victim needing others' attention? Are we supportive and caring of our co-workers or competitive, critical and mistrustful? Do we keep score, always noting who is giving more? Do we feel free to say what we think and what we want?

Our relationships with men and woman

Do we trust men more than women? Do we need a man, or a women, to prove we are worthy or powerful? Is our relationship with men or women always seductive? How do we change our behavior when we are with men, with women? Do we have friends of both sexes?

How are we in romantic relationships? Do we find a partner for our self who is truly loving, supportive and nurturing of us, who loves us for who we are, and do we love this person for who they are? Or do we create superficial relationships in which we can never speak our thoughts or feelings because it's dangerous? Are we always finding fault with them, or do we only see the positive so there is no balance in our view of them? Is there abuse or addiction involved? Do we want to transform this person? Are we possessive, jealous or blaming and call this love? Do we betray our love, do they betray us? Do we want this person to live for us or do we want to live through them? Or do we stay with this person only so we won't feel lonely?

How do we relate sexually? Is it an expression of our love and respect for each other? Can we be free to express our sexuality fully and freely? Can we talk about what we want, what feels good right now, and feel heard? Do we expect the other to intuit our needs and desires so any lack is their fault and not our responsibility? If we are sexually attracted to people of the same sex, do we feel free to express and enjoy our love? Is love good and sex dirty so we have to go outside of our love relationship for sexual excitement? Are we compulsive about sex—addicted to it to prove something or feel something? Is sex an obligation—we know it's important even if we don't always want it? Or do we think that sex is not important so we deny our self sexual expression, connection and fulfillment? Or are we disconnected from our sexuality and shut down to feeling?

Our relationships with children

How do we care for and relate to children—ours and others around us? Can we experience their uniqueness and beauty? Do we enjoy having fun with them or do we feel ridiculous, that it's a duty? Do we treat them as cute little objects, spend a few minutes with them and then push them aside? Do we feel a need to love them, a need to buy things for them? Are they too much for us—too much noise, too much open feeling, too much energy? What are our expectations of children? Can we allow them to be children or must they be little adults? Do we keep our self childless? Are we unworthy of them? Do we fear what we might do as parents? Do we shame, humiliate and punish our children just as our parents did with us?

Our relationship with work, authority and money

Do we enjoy our work, feel a sense of achievement and satisfaction? Do we believe in our abilities to accomplish and create? Or is work a sacrifice, a duty, a chore to be endured, and we complain but never change? Do we need work to prove our worth, to create our identity, to feel OK? Do we put all of our love, energy and time into our work so there is nothing else? Are we addicted to it? Are we afraid of work, perhaps we don't trust our ability to work so we are dependent on others? Are we mothers and homemakers who can't acknowledge that what we do is work?

How do we relate to authority? Can we listen and learn, benefit from the direction, recognize the value and respect authority? Or do we fear it, place our self in competition with it, challenge and undermine it? Do we rebel against it and feel superior because we can put authority down? Do we escape from it whenever possible? If we are authority our self, how do we treat others? Do we have to keep others below us? Do we fear anyone who knows more than we do? Do we humiliate others? Or are we afraid of being an authority— afraid of the responsibility, and so we lose out on many opportunities?

Do we know the true value of money and don't identify with it, so we can have it and use it beneficially for our self and others? Or is money all important in our life—the more money we have, the better we are? Does money equal security so we cannot spend it on our self or others in the present, but compulsively save for the future? Or do we spend it all and more so we are always in debt no matter how much we earn? Do we deny its value and keep ourselves with too little so we are worried all the time if we have enough? Do we denigrate the importance of money and spend others' money freely? Do we use money to buy attention and love from our lover, children, friends, siblings or our parents?

Our perspective on the world

When we meet new people, do we want to learn who they really are? Do we approach them with openness, trust and curiosity—a sense of adventure? Do we feel free to be who we really are and speak from our feelings and thoughts without fear of rejection? Or are we closed and fearful, seeing new people as potential danger? Do we look at them and judge them before they've even spoken? Or do we feel shame because we fear what they think of us? Do we try to be superior, or inferior? Are we seductive because of our fears of being rejected? What are our prejudices? Our prejudices and our transferences keep us from seeing people for who they are. Our eyes are closed to reality and we only see what fits our preconceptions; in fact, we can see what is not there, so we can never know the person.

Do we have a sense of community, a sense of belonging-ness in the world? Can we create and feel connected to a group that goes beyond our family? Can we relate to others as equals, learning and sharing with each other, having fun together and enjoying each other? Or do we feel lost in a group, not knowing where we stand? Do we fear judgment, rejection or danger? Can we tolerate and accept differences in people and nurture them wherever they are in life? Or do we need people to agree with us to feel safe?

How do we view the world? Do we see it as full of life and adventure, and we are eager to go out into it and learn about it? Do we marvel at the beauty of nature and experi-ence the weather as wonderful? Or do we feel that the world is hostile, our enemy, full of danger and threats? Are we afraid to go out without someone with us? Do we move in the world always protecting our self from attack? Is it "us against the world?"

How we bring fun, play and leisure into our life

Does play and fun have an important place in our daily life or is it relegated to last place after all the work is done? Is it limited to TV? Do we have to spend our free time in planned activities achieving some goal or can we be sponta-neous, flowing with our feelings and wishes in the moment? Do we have to be doing things? Is all of our leisure time spent with others or can we enjoy being alone? Or is fun and feeling good the most important thing in our life, and everything else suffers as a result?

Our resistance to knowing

For many of us it's hard to make even this limited inventory. We want to shift the focus because we don't want to know, it hurts too much or we can't remember. We feel our resistance to our self, our rejection of our reality. These patterns of denial were learned in childhood from our mother and father, directly from them or in reaction to them. Perhaps they were always pointing out our faults so we avoid looking at them. Some of us revel in the list-making of our negativities out of the same programming. We are experts at finding fault. Identifying the specifics of what is wrong with our life, and how we learned to be that way in childhood from our parents, clarifies the specific patterns, and their source in negative love. If we learned them, we can change them. Hope that change is possible moves us to commit to change, even though we don't know how.

Support for our journey

In healing our self it's valuable for us to have someone to guide us, to give us direction and support, especially when the going gets rough. In order to heal our past we have to connect with our inner emotional child who holds our shame, our pain and our anger, who holds our memories. It can be frightening to go there alone. We are vulnerable and afraid. Our patterns may tell us that at our core we are bad, flawed, defective, that the patterns are all there are and without them we will cease to exist.

There are negative, hurtful experiences and learned patterns, but there is no badness in us. Our intellect has worked hard to protect us from the pain, to keep it repressed and contained, but is has also kept us from our essence, our spirit. We need to experience our truth to know it. To do this work our intellect needs to move aside. We need to feel safe to surrender to our deepest feelings and memories so we can reclaim the wisdom within. A coach, teacher or therapist can create the psychic space and provide the support we need to go deep, to go into the places that feel too scary to go alone, to stand against our patterns. They can validate our perceptions, keep directing us to our inner wisdom, support us in being who we really are and point out truths about our experiences that we cannot perceive alone.

Committing to change

The work that we need to do to free ourselves from our negative patterns and reclaim our positivity begins in our intellect, with awareness. But most of our wounds happened long before the intellect was fully active. They happened on a physical and emotional level and that's where we have to go to heal them. Our intellect can understand the facts, but it cannot heal the pain. Our intellect, despite its many strengths, is stuck in its compulsive programming, and is keeping the rest of us stuck. All of our negative patterns are a result of our unconscious belief that our parents are the source of all love and knew best.

The way to achieve deep and lasting change is experientially. We reed to reconnect with our hurtful childhood experiences, and discover, validate and express our deepest feelings. We must re-experience our own essence, our spirit, and touch again that abundant, limitless source of love with which we were conceived. We are not our programming. We've lived defined by false beliefs too long. We need to experience fully our own truth so that we will know our truth rather than only believe it is so.

Change requires action. First we need awareness, then we must choose to act. We have lots of patterns about change— for example, it's difficult, slow, doesn't happen, doesn't last. Our patterns are flawed beliefs which limit and contain us, and keep us small and disconnected. Commitment has power in it. The act of committing to change actually sets change in motion.

Each step of the journey requires commitment to change, to let go of the past and move forward into the present where life is.

3

Acknowledging
Our
Essence

*Compulsive patterns disrupt our connection
with our essence which is love. Re-experiencing
and acknowledging that our spiritual essence
is love reveals our patterns as separate from us
and opens us to our inner wisdom. We can
envision living from our truth. We are
empowered to proceed from strength
rather than weakness.*

We have throughout our life experienced glimpses of our own spiritual essence, flashes of illumination and clarity. At these moments we felt connected, at peace, loved. We felt blessed. These experiences are treasures in our memory and we may yearn to return to that space. Many of us have searched diligently throughout our life for a deep and lasting connection with our spirit.

In childhood when we were not seen for who we really are, when our unique essence was not reflected back to us, we altered our image to try to please our parents, to win their attention and earn their love. In that process we lost sight of our spirit. We learned from our parents not to honor this vital aspect of our self, to ignore it, deny it. In this way negative love has kept us from a consistent experience of our spirit, the part of us that is eternal and divine.

Spirit embodied

Some say we are human beings having occasional spiritual experiences. Another view is that we actually are spirits who have taken on physical bodies to experience and learn things that are impossible on the spiritual plane, that we are spirit embodied.

Those who have had near-death experiences report being enveloped in a magnificent, loving, white light which radiates peace, serenity, acceptance and unconditional love. Often a being comes forth to greet them and give them guidance and support. They feel totally present in the moment. They feel loved. They see their life in a broader perspective. This experience of enlightenment and truth often transforms them. They have experienced how illusory this physical life is and lose their fear of death. Their values and behavior change. They feel spiritually awakened and more alive.

Even those who have had near-death experiences don't actually know what will happen when they do die. At most they've experienced only the first moments, the possibilities. In fact, none of us know what will happen when we die, although we have created and found belief in many scenarios. Even if we deny God, we can't deny the mystery of life and of creation. Medical science has not been able to pinpoint the moment of death. Perhaps this is because there is no point; rather a process that shades from life to death. Our life force cannot be defined by the chemicals in our body. It's energy, and energy doesn't disappear, rather it's transformed from one state to another. Death then could be the disconnection of our life force from our body, whereby our body becomes lifeless. And our essence, our spirit, lives on.

Imagine that when we were conceived our spiritual essence slipped into our body and our body became one with our spirit, totally connected to the spiritual realm. Some say that babies are still aware of their connection to the divine within and beyond and sleep in God's arms. There are many stories about small children experiencing a divine presence.

Programming alters our spiritual connection

It could be that in our early years we have access to both the spiritual world and life in the body, and almost imperceptibly a gradual transition occurs. Our programming lures us away from knowledge of where we were before and who we are. When this happens we no longer know that the divine is in us and is a part of us. We have lost touch with our self and thus we cannot reach out at will and touch the God beyond.

From our earliest childhood we have been made to feel,

in subtle and direct ways, that what we are inside isn't good enough, that something is wrong with us, that we are bad. Our parents warned us that "God can see what you're doing and will make you pay for it," placing God not only outside, but like a person, critical, blaming and vindictive. The way we were taught respect for God often instilled fear, that God demands certain behaviors and achievements, that God does not approve of who we are, that God punishes. We feel separate and learn to hide from God—to hide our feelings, our thoughts, our deeds. We become possessive and controlling. We claim that our God is better than others, championing sides and diminishing what God is.

We grow up disconnected from our spirit. We may attempt to reconnect spiritually. We've been taught rituals to bring us closer to God. We've been asked to believe. We've created marvelous pageantry with music, offerings and sacrifices. We spend hours in prayer and meditation. We work to find God through service. We try in a myriad of ways to reach out and experience again what once was ours.

In negative love we learn that God is outside of us and this is true, but not the whole truth. Our powerful positive essence, our unique spirit, is buried under layers of negativity. Some of us even deny it exists. We need to dig it out from this prison we unknowingly created for it. We need to create space for it to expand to its rightful size in our life. We need to reclaim it as our spirit that came from and is part of the universal intelligence. It's us and it goes beyond us. It connects us to the universe. Intellectually, emotionally and physically we need to expel the negativities and open our self to experience this aspect of us which is of divine origin. Then we can know the uniqueness and wonder of our true spirit.

Our spiritual essence is love. It is abundance. It is our

inner wisdom and the source of our creativity. It is light and reaches for transcendence. It is attracted to the source of all life from which it came. It is connection. It is divine.

Experiencing our spirit

We may expect that we have to rid our self of negativity before we can experience our spirit. This would, of course, require that once again we live on faith. But we don't have to wait. We can experience this magnificent aspect of our self through visualization. Visualizations are widely used today as powerful tools for growth and change. For example, in medicine visualization is used to invoke our internal powers of healing, in sports to enhance and strengthen our physical preparation and in business to create vision.

Visualizations have two parts: projective and receptive. If we tell our self to imagine a tree in front of us, we notice its color, size and special characteristic. We touch is leaves, its bark, and smell the flowers. The projective part of the visualization is that we told our self to imagine a tree. But we imagined our own specific tree, and often if we try to change the kind of tree that comes into our mind we can't. This part of the visualization is the receptive part that comes from our unconscious mind. It brings us images, feelings and messages that our conscious mind doesn't control. Visualizations allow us to tap into our unconscious and experience our inner truth.

In visualizations we can move outside of our negative programming and discover our loving, wise essence within. We can imagine and experience our self being enfolded and drawn up into a loving light beam. We can feel the love, peace and comfort of the eternal light of the universe fill our being and know that we are at one with the light. We can visualize our own spiritual essence and know that it is positive and strong. We can experience that we are love, and that this loving light is our home. Experiencing our spirit illuminates our illusions about power, achievement and possessions and brings perspective and meaning into our life.

Welcoming a spirit guide

In the light we can also call forth a spirit guide, a wise being who is present for us at every moment. We can experience this wise being greeting us with love, acceptance and nurturance. Our spirit guide is dedicated to our well-being and has the qualities needed to guide us on our journey back to our self. We can communicate with our guide whenever we want, asking for guidance, direction and support. Whenever we call on our guide, he or she will be there if we are open to listen. The responses often just appear in our mind.

Creating a sanctuary

With our guide we can go to a lovely natural setting in the sunshine which radiates peace and security and is ours alone. This serene mind space is always available to us. It is our own private sanctuary and is exactly the way we want it to be. It is a place of rest, meditation and learning.

Each of us has our own unique experiences of these visualizations. For some it is totally involving and awe-inspiring, for others of us the images are at first transitory and fleeting—our patterns interfering with the intensity of the experience. Regardless of our individual patterns, we can experience the light within and around us and know that it exists. This is a profound spiritual adventure that is beyond and outside of religion or disbelief. We experience the ocean into which all rivers flow. It is spirit and it is us.

We continue our journey into love acknowledging our essence, in touch with our spirit and our true potential. Knowing who we really are reveals our patterns as separate from us and gives us courage to proceed. We are working from our strength rather than our weaknesses. We see our negative patterns and the life created as a result of them with greater clarity. We can envision living from our truth. We can transfer our dependence from our intellect onto this core aspect of our being which is our inner wisdom and knowingness. This knowledge releases us from the denial that limits our choices and moves us along the path to freedom.

4

Getting
the Anger
Out

*To escape the hurt, fear and abandonment we
felt as a child, we got angry. Suppressed and
denied, that anger from our childhood surfaces
today as resentment, depression, illness and
violence. By focusing our anger's expression at
the source of the pain, we move the parents of
our childhood outside of us, establish clear
boundaries and claim our self.*

E ach of us has anger stored inside of us as a result of our childhood. Often we can't afford to acknowledge the anger, or its source, because we don't know what to do with it. For most of us, as children, it was never all right to express our anger. So we learned to stuff it down inside of us, and there it has been festering for all the decades since. Some of us have only a few conscious memories of that anger. Others of us have remained more aware. Unfortunately, the anger doesn't just go away. We have to recognize it for what it is, and we need to get it out of us.

The anger started with pain caused in our childhood by our parents. As we have discussed, even if our parents had wonderful intentions, they were not perfect. They were human. They acted in ways that hurt us. If our parents were neglectful and abusive, then our pain is even greater. Because of the things that our parents did to us or didn't do for us, at times we felt hurt, humiliation, guilt, shame, sadness, fear, rejection and abandonment. We felt invalidated for who we were, never good enough, wrong and unlovable. We felt confused and frustrated. We felt violated and abused. We may have felt, at times, that these could not be our real parents, we must have been adopted. These are all painful feelings.

We started experiencing these painful feelings in our mother's womb, and the pain continued to accumulate all through our childhood, building upon itself. The pain meant alienation from our parents. We had to find a way to try to reconnect. Each time we felt hurt as a child, we adopted a new negative love pattern or reinforced an existing one in an attempt to reconnect. When we felt our pain, we felt helpless and powerless because we felt alienated not only from our parents, but from our self, our essence, from our own inner strength and wisdom.

Often the pain was too great, we felt too powerless, so we moved away from the pain into anger. Anger gave us a sense of power. It gave us a sense of separation and distance from the hurtful person, our parent. When we expressed this justifiable anger to our parent, we usually learned quickly that it was not acceptable. And since we were absolutely dependent on them, it felt like we could not survive if we were alienated from them. So we learned to repress our anger, hide it or deny it. We were stuck between rejection and need.

We may have learned to alternate, to flip-flop, between repressing our anger and acting it out. Possibly in anger we were self-destructive and as a result got negative attention from our parents. Negative attention is preferable to no attention at all—at least we are seen—so we learn to turn our anger toward our self and be self-destructive over and over again to find connection.

It's like each one of our negative love patterns is anchored in us with pain and anger. The pain is a direct result of our parents' actions which caused us to feel alienated and adopt the pattern. The anger is directed toward them because they could not accept us for who we are.

Repressed feelings distort reality

Children have a right to all of their feelings. They have a right to be angry and express that anger toward their parents. The feeling of anger is a sign that something is wrong, that we have been hurt, that our boundaries have been violated. The expression of anger is a demonstration of hope that things can change. When our parents denied us the right to our anger, they diminished our hope that change can occur.

Since our survival depended on feeling loved by our parents, we could not stay conscious of the cause of the pain or the anger. So we repressed it, ignored it, even denied it. Many of us actually saw this repression of feeling being modeled by our parents. And in repressing the anger, we turned it against our self. We are the ones who suffer still.

Repressed anger actually changes the chemistry in our body. Directed inward at our self, it creates depression and self-destruction, patterns which are passed down from generation to generation as a result of negative love. Depression is rampant in our world. It's estimated that 18 million Americans suffer from depression right now. A significant proportion of the American public depends on anti-depressants to make it through the day. Suicide and self-destruction are on the rise, especially in young people. Our bodies endure the consequences of repression in all sorts of aches, pains, chronic illnesses and addictions. Think of how many of us suffer from tension headaches, back pain, stiff necks, high blood pressure, colitis, heart ailments, and even cancer. Alcohol, drugs and other additive substances and behavior help to deaden the pain. Our repressed anger is killing us metaphorically and actually.

Repressed childhood anger directed outward towards others manifests in resentment, vengeance and violence. Child abuse and spousal abuse are growing. Random acts of violence are on the increase. Many teens don't expect to make it into adulthood. Many of us feel like walking volcanoes waiting to explode. Vendettas continue beyond the time when anyone can remember their origin. Wars never seem to end. Killing sprees are triggered suddenly in people who have been model citizens until then.

All of us have experienced this repressed historical anger

as an adult. It happens on the highway when someone cuts us off and we explode in a rage, perhaps giving the driver "the finger" or even racing ahead to cut them off, placing our self and the others in our car in danger. And we feel justified, self-righteous. This reaction is so prevalent that is has been given a name, "road rage."

All of the justifiable anger that we could never express fully to our mother and father finds a seemingly acceptable excuse to come forth and temporarily release the pressure within. This happens most frequently when we are tired and under stress. Our target is often the ones we are closest to— our lover, child, friend, neighbor, boss, client, colleague. They ask us for something, or don't do what they said they would, and this torrent of anger comes gushing forth out of proportion to the event.

This is the way it's always been for us, maybe also for our mother and father (a direct adoption of a pattern) so we think it really is justifiable. Some anger might be appropriate, but not the intensity that comes forth. Our anger toward our parents as children is justifiable, but our repression of it has compounded its force and misdirected its expression.

Acknowledging our pain

We feel pain in our adult life. We need to connect that pain back to its origin in childhood with mother and father, to see the ways they hurt us and the hurtful patterns we learned. We need to identify the patterns that are keeping us in pain in our adult life. We need to connect with the anger that the pain has created and which we hold inside of us.

Many of us have had difficulty acknowledging this repressed anger. Our childhood programming holds the denial of pain and anger in place. First of all, as children we saw our parents as powerful, as all-knowing and wise, because we were totally dependent upon them and needed their love to survive. We had to deny their negativities or blame them on our self. Secondly, most of us were taught to honor our mother and father, and we came to believe this meant never questioning them, it meant agreeing with them and being like them. This is a very strong admonition for a little child, especially if it is also connected to the threat of permanent separation from mom and dad in the hereafter. Actually the act of honoring our parents means respecting them for who they truly are, allowing them to be human, to be imperfect, to be themselves. In fact, we dishonor our parents when we treat them as if they had to be perfect and refuse them their humanity.

Most of us can remember one or two things that happened in our childhood that hurt or angered us. This is a beginning. Some of us can remember numerous occasions when we were angry. When we recall those memories, we touch the anger again and know that it is still there, that it has always been there, that it is real.

So many of us remember very little of our childhood. This is not a sign of joyous, loving experiences. This repression of memories is a sign of pain and unhappiness. We repress what is too painful to know. Guided meditations and visualizations are wonderful ways to reclaim childhood memories and feelings. It can be valuable for us to have support and guidance in doing this so that it safe for us to remember what we have been repressing for so long, and we can be assisted in dealing with whatever painful memories might surface.

Our mind is a wonderful thing. In childhood it protects us from pain too hurtful to remember, and then in adulthood it brings forth the memories when we are strong enough and have adequate support to deal with them. When the childhood memories of hurtful experiences resurface in our adulthood, we can gather the resources to learn and grow, if we so choose.

In our childhood we had to deal with the trauma alone and helpless, but now we can choose to protect and help our self by working with a guide who can lead us through whatever darkness there is into the light of our own truth. It was not our fault and we are not to blame. Our intellect may know that, but our child can benefit from support in reclaiming the feelings once again.

Our internalized parents limit our life

Once we have identified what's wrong in our current life and gone back to our childhood and found the childhood experiences that created those negative love patterns, we know that we have adopted our parents' behaviors, moods, attitudes, admonitions (the shoulds and the shouldn'ts) and beliefs. We have taken our parents into our self, internalized them and become just like them. This realization is powerful, especially when we experience how we have become our parents in the ways we swore we never would. This knowledge can fuel our determination to be free of them so we can be our true self. Our parents do not belong in us, they fill up our space so there is no room for us. It is only by getting them out of us that we can become who we really are, that we can realize our true potential.

The parents of our childhood are held in us by the need for their love. This is the need of our inner child. This need can never be fulfilled. Childhood is past and we can't go back and change it. It was the way it was. Our parents have grown older, or died. This need cannot be filled by our parents now, although we keep hoping it can. It can only be realized by our re-connection to our inner essence, our spirit who is love. The negative parents of our childhood that we have internalized and look to for salvation are actually a barrier to the love we seek, which is in our own essence.

The parents who live in us and control our adult life through their patterns, regardless of how strongly we rebel, are creations of our own need. They are a powerful illusion that we created in childhood whose continued existence is dependent on our belief that they are us. But they are not us. Our parents and their patterns are separate from us. Once we have experienced our spirit, we can know that we have an identity separate from them.

Creating a boundary through expression

We must destroy the internalized parents of our childhood who parasitically live in us—they will not leave on their own. They are our creation and remain trapped within us as we experienced them in childhood. We must sever the ties we created. We must disconnect from the need for their approval and love which they can never give. Disconnecting is a challenging task, but it is the way to draw a boundary between us and our parents—to get them out of our being.

This work must be done by our inner emotional child who has been carrying all the pain and anger. Our child must reclaim its voice and speak its truth. It takes courage, commitment and a safe environment for expression. This task cannot be accomplished intellectually, spiritually or only physically, but we need the support of our body, spirit and intellect.

We focus on one parent at a time having already identified the patterns that we learned from him or her. Our emotional child expresses its hurt and anger out loud at that negative internalized parent of our childhood for all that parent did to us, didn't do for us, for all the patterns he or she taught us. We express all the anger that has been stored in us since childhood for each individual painful act of our parents, and for the damage those negative patterns have done in our adult life.

Anger for anger's sake accomplishes nothing. Our expression of anger needs to be focused on the cause of the anger. We need to disconnect from the specific patterns and give them back to the internalized parent one by one. We empower our child to do and say things that were not permitted in childhood, such as yelling, screaming, and swearing, making as much noise as it wants. We tell our parents that the negative patterns are not us, the patterns are theirs and we refuse to be identified with them anymore. We disown them. We throw our internalized parents out of us, get rid of them, destroy them and claim our independence to be who we really are.

As we do this feeling work, this physical work, expressing the anger that we have held and denied for so long, we start to feel the freedom to express what was for all our life inexpressible. We experience the power of shouting our truth. Yes, it really hurt us! The memories start coming back faster because now there's a purpose in remembering. It's not just feeling the pain again. Expressing the pain and anger is freeing us from it. We revel in our reclaimed ability to state our truth. We claim our life as our own.

Our energy shifts as we disconnect
We feel the burden lifting. Our energy shifts, and we know that we have destroyed the power of our internalized

parent over us. They are dead and we are free. Despite all the exhausting work, suddenly we feel full of energy. We feel light and joyous. Our facial expression changes, becomes more real, more approachable, our eyes are clear. Our body is more alive. We are freed from the need to be like our parents, to earn their love.

By getting our anger out of us, we move our parents into their rightful place outside of us. We are no longer merged with them. We have our own clear boundaries. We know that we are not our parents. We are not their negative patterns. They no longer live in us. We have experienced our separation from them. We have more space in our life for our essence. We know our spirit is our essence. It's true—we are better than we thought we were.

This is a gigantic step in our journey.

5

Finding Forgiveness and Compassion

Having released our anger, our path takes us into the reality of our parents' childhoods. Deep emotional understanding of their lives brings forgiveness, and compassion for the child that lives in each of them. In giving them unconditional love, we can finally experience compassionate forgiveness and love for our self.

When we have moved our parents into their rightful place outside of us, for the first time in our life we have the ability to gain a broader perspective on *their* lives. In experiencing our own reality, our own truth, we gain the ability to experience the whole truth – not just our truth, but also our parents' truth. We have the opportunity to perceive our parents for who they are, separate from us, separate from our need for them to love us.

Even if we think we know their truth, we know it primarily intellectually. Perhaps we've justified what they've done—we feel they did the best they could. But our emotional understanding has been blocked by our repressed hurt and anger toward them. Our unconscious resentment of our parents has limited our ability to experience deep, heartfelt understanding. Our inner child held on to blame, covertly if not overtly, because our parents could not love us the way we needed to be loved. Maybe we even blamed our self for not being able to love them in the way they deserved.

Having freed ourselves of our repressed negative feelings at our internalized parents through expressing those feelings, we can connect once again with our ability to look at the truth, to understand emotionally and give up blaming. We know that they were guilty for all the hurtful things they did to us. Now we are able to experience what their childhood was like, and understand what drove them to be the way they were. Then we can know that they were not to blame.

We may be fearful of losing our hard-won power if we look at their side. This is understandable. All during our childhood our parents were powerful and we felt powerless. They've been up and we've been down. In expressing our hurt and anger, we have won freedom *from* them. But there's a catch. Protest is always co-dependent because it's always *against* others. We are still negatively attached. In protest we derive our power from putting others down—now we're up and they are down. That change feels good. We don't want to lose this power we've gained. But in protest our focus is on others—on keeping them down, keeping them powerless. It is competitive, and requires vigilance. We must always be protecting our self from attack .

The final goal is freedom *for* our self so we can know our self and live our own life. And allow the others to live their lives without judgment. We can achieve that freedom through seeing both sides. Only when we see our self as we really are, and see the others as they really are, can we be whole and truly free.

We do not do this for our parents, we do this for us. It is the way to go beyond the superficial power of superiority and condescension, and find our inner power. To free our self from negative love, we first must find deep emotional understanding, forgiveness and compassion for our parents. In doing this, we open our self to finally experiencing forgiveness and compassion for our self. We can free our self from the reactivity of negative love which compels generation after generation to replay the same debilitating scenarios.

Our parents also were driven by negative love

The truth is that our parents were once little babies, too. It may be hard for us to imagine them as babies because when we were born they were already adults. But our mother once was a small girl, and our father was a little boy. They had parents who couldn't give unconditional love to them and all their life they have yearned to be loved just like we have. They learned all their negative patterns in their childhoods, and then they didn't have any choice but to pass them on to us. They took on their parents' behaviors, moods, attitudes and beliefs just like we did, in order to try to earn their parents' love. They experienced their own childhood traumas. They made decisions to be different from their parents. They too suffered from the burden of negative love. In truth they did the very best they could. They may have even given us more than they received themselves.

If our mother or father was submissive, critical, violent, abusive, controlling, abandoning, cold, distant, a victim, they learned all these patterns with their mother and father. If they really had a choice, they wouldn't have chosen a life like theirs. And we wouldn't have chosen to be the way we have been in our life.

Deep down our parents were driven by a need for love and acceptance—some sense that they were all right. They couldn't get what they needed from their parents and as a result couldn't accept or love themselves. Then they weren't able to love us or get the love they wanted from us, although they may have tried. If a parent has died, they may have gone to their grave without ever feeling loved and accepted. And if they are living, they may still feel unloved and unappreciated. They may feel that they have missed out on a large portion of their life.

All our life we have made assumptions about who our parents are. Often our parents have told us stories about their childhood and we have believed them all true. Remember now the stories we have told others about our childhood, and compare those stories to the truths we have uncovered in getting our anger out. Usually there is some serious discrepancy, if not in fact, then in completeness.

Experiencing our parents' childhoods

We need to awaken our curiosity about what our parents experienced in their childhood and our desire to learn who they really are. We must open our hearts to their hearts, to explore what they felt as children with their parents. We need to put the blame aside, go beyond it to deep emotional understanding. We need to be willing to walk in their shoes and experience what their life was like for them.

Just as we have an emotional child within us that has been hurt and loveless all our life, our parents also have an emotional child within them that has not been loved, and carries pain and sadness. The next challenge in the journey is to get to know that hurt little child inside each of our parents.

We can do this by first connecting with our own inner emotional child and experiencing our heart open to our child. We feel the curiosity of our child about what our parents really experienced in their childhood. From that child within us, we imagine the child within our parents and allow our curiosity to invite that child of our parent into our presence. We sit together, two children of the same age, eager to talk with each other, to understand. We are tapping into our natural abilities to connect with the emotional experiences of our parent's childhood. In this state we can ask our parent's child anything we want about their childhood. They will answer us, if we are willing to listen and receive what they say without judgment.

This step is much different than getting the anger out. That was all about us and our pain. To experience our parent's life, we have to move outside our self, put our self aside, and focus on the other.

For those of us who have been caretakers, who have been

programmed to defend and protect others, this may feel more comfortable and be easier. Or we can resist because we fear falling back into those patterns. For those of us who have been self-absorbed, this experience may feel alien and foolish and we may find all of our defenses up against it. For those of us with strong, skeptical intellects, this step may feel ridiculous and impossible, or it may flow effortlessly.

Whether we struggle through this experience or it comes easily, we all discover that our parents suffered in their childhood just like we did, and very possibly much more than we did. The amazing thing about this inquiry is that if we check out the accuracy of the information we receive, including the surprising or even shocking parts, we discover the essence is accurate.

We need the information from the child in each of our parents to understand how they felt in their childhood, and how they learned their worst patterns from their parents. We need the details to grasp how they had no choice but to adopt the negative patterns. They were compelled to be as they were just as we were. Then we no longer are able to condemn them. When we reach this state, we find compassionate forgiveness for them.

Compassion opens us to our humanity

There are many definitions of compassion. One is that compassion is sorrow for the suffering of another, accompanied by a strong desire to alleviate the pain and remove the cause. Another definition is loving kindness. In Latin *compassio* means walking along side. Compassion is different than sympathy where we enter into another person's misery or pity, where we feel sorry for them. To give an illustration: a person falls into a hole and injures her leg. Sympathy would be jumping down in the hole with that person, perhaps harming our self, and sharing the misery. Pity might be looking down at their misfortune. Compassion would be throwing down a rope to pull them out of the hole so they can receive the care they need.

In actuality, we have been living our life in sympathy with our parents, sharing their misery. The source of our parents' suffering is that they didn't feel lovable and as a result they couldn't love us or receive love from us or from anyone. When we free our self from the pain in our life, which was created in reaction to our parents' inability to love, we are able to love freely. This frees our parents as well. They are no longer burdened by what they did to us, how their acts have limited us. We can also give our parents what they always wanted, unconditional love and acceptance for who they are, just as they are.

Only when we feel our separateness from our parents, when we find our own life, when we are in touch with our own inner source of love, can we express true, deep compassion. Compassion and forgiveness are our keys to freedom. They release us from the compulsivity and unconsciousness of negative love and enable us to move to the next level of growth. They enable us to feel our humanness, and the humanity of others—to walk along side them.

Expressing forgiveness and compassion

One way for us to experience and express our understanding, forgiveness and compassion for our parents is to imagine their death, as if it is happening in the present moment. We can do this whether they are currently living or have already died. This experience can free their souls from the debt they had to us and we had to them.

A parent's death is a great loss. Even if we hate them, fear them or disdain them, we have needed their love. Our parents carry the promise in our minds that, perhaps, some day they will love us in a way that will fill the need created in childhood. If they have already died, we feel the loss of this potential.

As we imagine holding our dying parents in our arms, we know that we want to repair and complete our relationship with them. We see the small child within each of them reaching out to us for love and understanding. We have many things to say to them and there is only a short time, so we must be direct and succinct. We tell each of them that we understand them now as we never have before. We don't condemn them anymore, and we have stopped condemning ourselves as well. We forgive them and feel deep compassion for them.

When our dying parents hear these words from us, they know it's safe to speak from their heart about how hard they tried to be good parents. Finally we can hear them. We can understand and accept who they are. We can accept what they say. We feel open to everything they gave to us, and understanding of everything they couldn't give. And we imagine them dying in our arms.

It is wonderful to make peace with those who gave us life. We give absolute forgiveness to them, and say all the things we couldn't say before. We free their souls. Finally, we can give our parents heartfelt unconditional love and acceptance for who they truly are. We no longer need to receive anything from them in return. We no longer need to try to earn their love. Now we can give just to give. This is a blessing.

In setting their souls free, we also free our self. We no longer need to hold onto them in pain or anger, guilt, blame, or out of need. Once we have freed them to be who they really are, we are free to be our self. We no longer go through life reacting to others as if they are our parents. We can be free of transference and finally experience others in our life for who they really are.

Death is a certainty. It will come to us as well. Imagine what our funeral will be like if we continue living our life in negative love—in reaction, unconsciously and compulsively. Imagine what our spouse, lover, children, siblings, co-workers, even our mother and father, would say and do if they could remove their mask of sociability and denial and say what they felt. What would they want to say to us about the pain, hurt and alienation we create? What would they say about what we did to them, to our self, and to others in our life?

Do we want to continue in negative love and go to our grave surrounded by so much anger, guilt, blame and debts? Or do we want to choose another life for our self where we can give and receive love, give and receive life, give and receive forgiveness, understanding and compassion?

We can choose how we will live our life—first with our self and then with people around us. If our mother and father are still living, we have the opportunity to develop a new and different relationship with them, not based on our need for their love or our guilt, but freely giving of love and compassion.

Compassion for our parents and for our self is a worthy accomplishment. It is the beginning of compassion, the ground floor. We are all human and imperfect. We were all programmed in our childhood. This is true not only for our mother and father and us, but for everyone everywhere. Everyone had a mother and father and learned everything from them, and they didn't have any choice in their life except to pass this on to their children. It is so easy to be blind to this reality. When we realize this truth, we change the way we perceive others. We change our view of humanity. We change our life. Compassion is a practice that requires consciousness and choice.

First we connect to our self, then we connect with our mother and father, then with people we love and live around, including our siblings, lover, children, friends and co-workers. We accept each person as a spirit who came from the light, and like us took on negativity in order to survive. We can recognize that the negative patterns they are compulsively acting out are what they learned from their parents would bring them love and connection. Knowing that each of us is a spirit embodied yearning to connect, we can have compassion and understanding of all humankind. We can experience the light in others. We can experience it in the world. We can experience it in every living thing. We feel our connection with people everywhere in the world today and throughout history. Then we know the unity of life and can connect even more deeply with God. In this way we can live from our spirit.

Once we have experienced compassion, forgiveness and love for our parents, and for our self, we feel more authentic, connected with our self, with all of humanity, and with God inside and outside of us. We feel at peace and in awe. We have ended our denial of death. Each day could be the last day of our life and we can live it to the fullest because acceptance of death is the door to life. Our step is lighter and our back straighter. We feel acceptance and love for ourselves. We feel open to give and receive without attachment. We feel full of love and gratitude.

6

Ending
the Battle
Within

*Freed from negative attachment to our
parents, we face the war within. The internal
battle between child and intellect has stressed
our body and obscured our spirit. Expressing
the grievances makes space for a truce, an
agreement to work together in partnership
and harmony, and create inner peace.*

By this point in the journey, we have expelled the negative parents within, and found understanding, forgiveness, compassion and love for our mother and father. But the battle within us rages on. Perhaps we can even hear our inner voices more clearly. That's good. Because now we are ready to look inside, at our four aspects, and deal with how we are holding the negative patterns within our self.

We are at war with our self. The voices we hear most are our emotional child and intellect, but there is also the body. Our child doesn't agree with our intellect, and our intellect doesn't agree with our child. And neither really listens to the body. They continually sabotage each other to get the upper hand. Each commands an army of negative patterns. They complain about the other, blame and shame each other and end up feeling alone and lonely with no one to trust or depend on.

For example, we have an important presentation to give at work. Our intellect is well prepared and pleased with the work we have done. As we start speaking our child's fear of criticism and rejection comes through in our shaking hands and voice. We feel divided, ungrounded and out of control. Or we see someone in a public place whom we love, and we want to give them a hug and kiss. Our intellect says, "If we do that, we'll embarrass them and they will be angry with us." Even if we go ahead and hug and kiss them, it's not the same. We feel the self-criticism, the fear and the caution. Or we have been overdoing, not getting enough sleep, not eating properly—pushing the edges. We get that awful flu that knocks us into bed and we feel betrayed by our body.

Sometimes the fighting stops and the child and intellect

collude with each other. This is always the case with addictions. For example, we may know that we abuse alcohol, but the child wants a drink to relax and enjoy its day off. After all it's Sunday. The intellect agrees. We have one drink, and then another, and another until we are drunk once again. The next day the intellect tries to escape all responsibility by blaming the child for coming up with the idea and the child blames the intellect for not stopping it. Our body suffers the consequences of a hangover, and additional damage to our liver.

The war between our child and our intellect is played out through our body. Our body is the battleground and pays the price over and over again. The patterns of our body, the ones it learned directly from our parents, contribute to the war—our stress, tension, nervousness, our exhaustion, illness, eating disorders such as anorexia and bulimia, smoking, drinking, illegal or prescription drugs, other addictions, chewing our fingernails, our frown or false smile, our posture, our seductiveness, our sexual inadequacies, our shame, our rages and tantrums. We don't listen to the messages that our body sends—discomfort, tiredness, stiffness, pain, sniffles—so the volume gets turned up. Our body is tired of the war.

As a result of the fighting, our spirit seems invisible. It's obscured by the negativity. There's no space for it on the battlefield. Even if it appears, it's swept aside by logic, fear or activity. At moments when the battle has stopped, we can sometimes experience our spirit and marvel in the peace it brings us. For most of us this is so infrequent in our lives and so special that we remember a moment like this for years. But we don't understand how to live from this peaceful space, or even get back here.

We may have learned to parent our wounded inner child. We can listen to it and validate its feelings. We let it know that we always want to be there for it as our parents never were. We are ready to defend it and care for it. This consciousness is rewarding. It brings relief from the loneliness. But re-sculpting our intellect into the good parent extends the innate inequality of the parent-child relationship. It's time to go beyond this limited relationship.

In truth, our emotional self is tired of being a powerless, hurt child who needs to be cared for by others. It wants to mature, become an adult, and take its rightful place as an equal partner along side our intellect and body.

Our intellect is tired of having to be in control and make decisions. It's tired of always having to be responsible and achieve. Our intellect wants to be heard and listened to. It wants a companion in life from whom it can learn, and with whom it can share responsibility and pleasure.

Our body is tired of being ignored, abused and denied. Our body is central to experiencing life. It has information and abilities we need to learn and grow—to live well. It deserves an equal place on the team with the intellect and emotional self.

Just as we had to get out all of the anger at our parents, we now have to recognize and express all the thoughts, feelings and judgements that our intellect, child and body have about each other, and about the spirit. There needs to be a clearing where it is all expressed and heard.

Complaints our intellect has about our child

Our intellect has had to try to make sense out of every-thing, even feelings. A tremendous amount of programming took place before our intellect was active. These patterns don't make sense. But our intellect has had to try to under-stand and explain them to us. It's no wonder it's defensive and cranky. Our emotional child has given little help to our intellect in untangling the mystery of why we are the way we seem. Our intellect has many complaints about our child. The intellect has to identify these complaints so that it can voice them and be heard.

Our child is needy, demanding and dependent, but it won't listen. Does it ignore and avoid what it doesn't want to deal with? Does it withdraw, act stupid, confused, distracted, spacey, or invoke drama, act the victim or martyr, throw temper tantrums? Is our child submissive on the outside and resistant within, acting the goody-goody to earn love while feeling resentful? Does it shut down, space out, and become a zombie? Is it angry, stubborn, and rebellious? Is it depressed? Does it state all of its feelings, or only the "good" ones repressing the "bad" ones so we never know what's going on? Does our child lie directly or through innuendoes? How does it manipulate and trick us? Is it ruled by fear and self-doubt, resistant to change and growth? How does it hold its grudges, like a badge of honor or tightly and secretly? Does the child play the clown, always out for a good time even to the point of self-destruction? Does it attract negative attention for its apparent inadequacies? Are we, intellect, always having to get it out of trouble, cover up its indiscretions? Is our child jealous of others, of us, intellect? Is it a defeatist always feeling, "I can't" or "This is too hard?" How seductive is our child? How does it seduce us? Is it self-indulgent? How does it blame and shame us? How does our child set it up to be rejected by us, intellect, or for us to be rejected by others?

Complaints our child has about our intellect
Our emotional child has actually suffered far longer than

our intellect. It was struggling to survive for years before the intellect became fully active, and then took over. It's rarely been really listened to by anyone including our own intellect. Our child's resentments need to be identified and expressed.

Our intellect is controlling and invalidating of our child. How does the intellect repress our feelings? Does it deny their existence or feel that feelings are a bother? Is it critical, judgmental, rigid and aloof? Is our intellect over-responsible or irresponsible, or does it flip-flop from one to the other? Does it indulge in magical thinking, expecting the desired solution to just appear? Is our intellect superior and above it all or inferior and inadequate? How does the intellect justify and rationalize the way it treats us? Did it ever really listen to our needs and gently but firmly help us understand? Our child didn't know any better when it adopted all those patterns and our intellect let us play out the patterns and then blamed us.

How seductive is our intellect, how does it seduce us? What part does it play in our addictions? How does it collude with us and then turn around, repudiate any responsibility and blame and shame us? How does it make us feel like we don't deserve anything, that we're unworthy? How does our intellect act as if it is our spirit, so self-righteous and knowledgeable with all the right words and behaviors? The intellect often believes that it always knows best. It denies reality and can even makes the negative positive. How does our intellect set itself up to be rejected and abandoned by us, child, and to be rejected by others in our life?

Complaints our child and intellect have about our body

Our child and intellect have been living with our physical body our whole life. They have many grievances about the body. They complain that the body as a whole and its various parts are the wrong size and shape, and the body needs so little food before it gains weight. The hair is the wrong color, and there's too little of it. The eyes are too small or too large, and can't see clearly. The face is falling, wrinkles forming, and the stomach sticks out. They are upset that the body is getting old, is not reliable anymore, that it doesn't move well, feels clumsy and inept. They are intolerant of the aches and pains, the hurts, the stiffness, the tightness, the closed-down feelings, the lack of stamina. Is the body unexpressive or unresponsive, shut down to feelings and desires, or over-expressive, constantly in motion, feeling that there is never enough activity? Does it get tired easily and need lots of sleep, or can it never seem to sleep well? Does it snore? Is it rigid creating a barrier between us and others? Are its appetites for sex, food, exercise, drugs, alcohol uncontrollable? Does it always get sick at inopportune times? Is it chronically ill, even jeopardizing life? Does our duality hate that our body is vulnerable to injury, stops functioning, and dies?

Complaints our body has about our duality of child and intellect

Our body has experienced all sorts of abuse from our duality of child and intellect, who resent being contained and limited by it. Our body must also claim its voice and speak up. Our duality needs to understand what's it's been doing to our body. Our duality of child and intellect has been treating our body like a machine that's supposed to run perfectly and endlessly, providing mobility, bringing pleasure and joy, and never feeling any pain.

Often the child has been stuffing feelings into the body so organs and muscles are sore, tense and tight. Or the child uses the body to throw tantrums, acting out indulgently and excessively. Do the child and intellect really listen to the body, nurture it and fulfill its needs? Or do they have their own agenda about what the body should be—its shape, size, appearance? Do they take risks with the body, incurring damage? Do they stuff it with food, drugs or alcohol and indulge in other addictive substances and activities? Does the duality ignore or deny the information our body sends of discomfort and comfort, pain and pleasure? Does our duality only wants to feel "good" things? Does it take pills to silence the body's messages, lose all sensation, then use something to simulate feeling? Our child and intellect treat the body as an object at their service.

The confrontation

Our complaint-filled emotional child, intellect and body are each like baskets overflowing with balls. The basket is so full of complaints that not even one more will fit. We can't take anything in. We can't learn. We need to empty out the entire basket. All of the complaints need to be spoken out loud in detail. In fact, they need to be yelled with energy and determination to finally be listened to and heard. First one and then the other says all there is to say. While one is speaking the others can do nothing but listen.

These confrontations are validating. We need to go back and forth saying all that's within us until we know that to continue blaming means we stay stuck and separate. Each aspect has a different perspective. By expressing all these thoughts and feelings out loud, we empty the baskets and prepare the way for healing. Our intellect learns from our child and our child learns from our intellect. Our child and intellect learn from our body, and our body learns from our child and intellect. Finally we can gain understanding of the others' experience, the others' perspective.

We realize that none of us is to blame. We need to forgive each other for the many things we have done in the past and find compassion for each other. Certainly if we can find compassion for our mother and father, we can find compassionate forgiveness for each of our aspects. It was all compulsive programming. Each of us has suffered from the same burden.

A truce

We need to end the battle and make a truce, an agreement to work together in collaboration, learn from each other and take care of each other. Unless we create an agreement to work together and live in harmony we are never going to find peace and love within our self.

In the truce, as the intellect, we agree to listen to and accept our feelings and not deny or suppress any of them, or invalidate our child for having them. We agree to take responsibility for our behavior. We agree to be patient with our child and lovingly identify our child's patterns and explain things simply and clearly until our child can understand. We agree to give support and direction to our child, and help our child so we can grow and learn together. We will involve our child in making decisions which benefit us all. Then when our child grows up and becomes a positive emotional adult with all its wonderful childlike qualities such as joy, spontaneity and laughter, our intellect and emotional self can become equal partners together.

As the child, in the truce, we agree to listen to and cooperate with our intellect and stop manipulating and controlling. We agree to communicate all our feelings and needs and to stop hiding any feelings, negative or positive. We agree to respect the intellect's ideas in the same way that the intellect agrees to respect our feelings. We will participate in making decisions that will be beneficial to our whole being. We agree to listen to our intellect when it lovingly points out our patterns. We recognize that our intellect is competent and knowledgeable, and we agree to trust it and learn and grow together as partners.

And our positive child and re-educated intellect together as partners need to come to a truce with our body. We agree to listen to our body's needs and care for it with respect and reverence. We agree not to cause our body any more distress. We will identify the patterns and free our body from them. We agree to enjoy our body's sensuality and movement in space, to express our sexuality lovingly, but not abuse it. We agree to feed our body healthy food and drink, and provide adequate rest and recreation.

Having made a truce between our child, intellect and body, we can experience our spiritual essence as a vital aspect of our being, not an illusion. We have cleared the space in our life for this vital life force to grow and flourish. Finally we can hear the messages it has for us in our life. Our spirit is no longer just a fleeting moment of illumination and peace; we can feel experience its presence whenever we choose. Now we can have balance in our life. We no longer need to deny it or be fanatical about it. Finally we can accept our spirit as an integral part of us, no more important than any of our aspects, but with its own unique place in our lives—the source of love, wisdom, creativity and connection.

In doing this experiential work we create peace in our being. We gain self-understanding and self-acceptance. We create space for our spirit to express its wisdom and its love.

The loneliness disappears and we feel loved and loving. We feel the relaxation and fullness of our body. We experience the quietness of our mind. We feel the harmony among our four aspects. We experience our sense of commitment to our self, our integration, and our peace. We hear the silence—the amazing blessed silence.

7

Moving
Beyond Blame

Finally we see that blaming our self and others keeps us negatively attached to the past and limits us to fantasizing a better future. We keep missing the moment. Moving beyond the compulsive blaming and desire for revenge restores our ability to live in the present with responsiveness and choice.

B efore we start this journey, our feelings are blocked and limited. In childhood we had to repress our anger and other "unacceptable" feelings. Unfortunately, when we repress one feeling, we affect them all because there is only one channel to our feelings. As a child we couldn't express anger and as a result we can't feel or express love. Our feeling channel became clogged with our fear, pain, guilt, shame, anger and vindictiveness.

In the beginning steps of this journey, we express and release many of these repressed feelings and clear a portion of the channel so our feelings can flow more freely. But there is more that we need to do to open the channel fully so we can live in the moment—so we are free to experience and express in the moment our authentic feelings (not our patterns) without judgment, and are free to be in the next moment to experience what is there. This is being present to our self, to our life, to others. This is positivity. It's not holding on to the feeling, examining it, enlarging or diminishing it, wishing we or someone else had done or said something different. Time never comes back again. No matter how hard we try, we cannot bring it back, just as we cannot return to our childhood and have it be the way we wanted it to be.

Our ultimate need is love. In negative love we feel disconnected and unloved. We feel that there is something innately wrong with us. So we abandon our self and adopt the patterns of our parents in an attempt to earn their love. We end up feeling more negative and unlovable. We achieve the opposite of what we strive for. We want love and we end up feeling unlovable. By adopting our parents' negativity and compulsively acting out their patterns, we set our self up to be abandoned over and over again.

Negative love is always vindictive

We hate being rejected and abandoned. It hurts and we feel bad! We feel resentful and look for someone to blame for the hurt. We learned that *someone* has to be at fault. We may blame our self, or we can look for someone outside our self to blame. We hang onto the grudge and try to get back at the person we blame. We hold the false belief that the only way to get rid of that hurt feeling is to get even, whether with our self or someone else—that's vindictiveness. Negative love is always vindictive.

Negative love builds a bridge which lifts us out of the present and keeps us commuting between the story of our past and the fantasy of our future, bypassing the present. We can't experience the present. We can only look upon it, observe it, and, perhaps, touch the surface. The only place that life really exists is in the present, in this moment. But in negative love the only apparent choices are to recreate the past or dream of a better future.

There are different ways we can hold on to the negative feelings inside of us, continue to set our self up to be rejected, and blame our self and others. First, we can determine that there are things in our life that we just cannot change, that we have been handicapped too severely to ever rectify. We give up hope, and resign our self to our perceived limitations. We wear the negativity as a mark, however subtle, of our victimization. This may be done unconsciously. But our parents, living or dead, and the world, can see from our life how bad they were. Or we deny the hurt of the past, repress it, act as though it is forgiven and forgotten. We create the illusion of happiness, success and love. We believe we have escaped. At moments, we feel the hollowness of the myth we have created, and blame our self. Or we create a fantasy about how perfect our life will be when we have moved into the magical future. Everything will be wonderful, and everyone will love us and we them. We will have what we want. In this way we set up unrealistic expectations for our self and others, which ensures that we will be frustrated and have justification to turn around and blame.

Vindictiveness grows on a base of self-righteousness. As a result of a perceived or real injustice to us, we feel justified in holding on to the blame, holding on to the past, and allowing it to shape our future. We feel hurt and we want someone to suffer. We want to get back at them. We want to prove that they were wrong and we were right. We want to get even. Look at that colloquialism: getting even—wanting to move to their level and be like them. If they hurt us, why would we want to be like them? It's perverse, and yet it's what we learned to do as a child with our parents. We felt abandoned by them, so we tried to be like them.

We have the false belief that life is fair. Life isn't about fairness. Life is about learning and growing. Life is change. Our need for vindication keeps us tied to the injustice and forces the injustice to direct our life. It keeps us limited and rigid. It keeps us the powerless victim while at the same time providing us the illusion of power. Often the person who has done the perceived or real injustice is oblivious to it, or has forgotten it and gone on with their life. We create and perpetuate our own victimhood.

Identifying our vindictiveness

Let's look at our life and determine how we are self-vindictive. How do we create the circumstances so that we feel compelled to reject our self, blame our self, get back at our self and justify our behavior? Are we a perfectionist, intolerant of any imperfection? How do we disparage our thoughts, feelings, actions? How do we criticize our body, our sensuality and our sexuality? How do we withhold pleasure from our self? How do we denigrate our abilities, our achievements, our vision? How do we act in a self-destructive manner? What are our addictions? How many times have we thought it would be better if we were never born or if we died? How many times have we considered suicide or attempted it, directly or indirectly?

How are we vindictive to others in our life? How do we set it up to reject others so they reject us and then we blame them, and want to get back at them? Do we do it with criticism, abuse, violence, or by withdrawing and withholding? How do we do it with our parents, our spouse or lover, our children, our siblings, our friends, our boss, our co-workers, acquaintances, storekeepers, careless drivers? Are we covert, using sarcasm, joking, being too busy or withholding attention or love? Do we act on it or just think about it? Do we hope that the universe will right the wrong and then feel even more self-righteous because we have not dirtied our hands?

Rather than learning, growing and changing, we are stuck in blaming—trapped by our vindictiveness. First we blamed our self. That was the start of negative love. We felt an absence of love and blamed our self for what was missing, and then changed our self to be like our parents to try to reconnect. When it didn't work, we blamed our self more. As we grew, we became capable of noticing that mother and father weren't God, and we blamed them. We saw that others weren't perfect either, and blamed them. Then we realized that the universe isn't fair and we blamed God.

We need to look at how we have complained about God, or been afraid to complain. Have we questioned and blamed God all our life? Perhaps we covered it up because it wasn't acceptable. How often have we said, "It isn't fair?" Have we asked, "Why are there inadequate and hurtful parents? Why are there starving children, diseases, disasters?" Have we felt inferior and without dignity? How often have we called for help and felt our prayers weren't answered? We may even deny that God exists. What image do we have of God? Is it an old man with a beard and flowing gown who is watching us all the time, looking for mistakes and blaming us, just like a parent? Is our God vindictive? Do we fear punishment if we say or do or think the wrong thing? Do we try to keep secrets from God while at the same time thinking God is omnipotent? Are we afraid to speak our truth to God? Do we pray only from fear, guilt, or when we want something? How distant have we felt from God and from our spirit?

Regardless of our religion, what kind of relationship do we have with God? All of our negative patterns are barriers to the spirit who lives within us and around us. We can't grasp God intellectually and logically, and we blame God. We conceptualize God as if God is another person. But God is bigger than we can conceive within our mind. We cannot find words to contain the essence of love, compassion or God no matter how hard we try. Some of us have dedicated our life to spirituality, but we can't feel God within us, and we feel frustrated. We pray for hours each day, and then treat our loved ones badly or ignore the homeless. We condemn and reject others who approach spirituality differently than we do. We may find a spiritual master and try to make that person into God. We develop a spiritual practice, but stay disconnected from the spirit in us and others. Or we deny God completely.

Unspoken vindictiveness is vicious because it lives forever in our mind. We can deny it, ignore it, repress it, but it seeps out and poisons our relationships. And we can't understand why. Vindictiveness targets vulnerability and weakness. It seeks the tender spots most sensitive to attack in those with power to hurt us. It is sadistic. It waits and watches for the right moment, the perfect opportunity to strike. It wants to destroy. It finds a way to deliver the blow. We have done it to our self. We have done it to our spouse or lover. We do it to our parents, our children, our friends, authorities, strangers. Vindictiveness keeps us smaller than we are. It keeps us separate. It makes us afraid of our self. It alienates us from our spirit.

Releasing vindictiveness through its expression

To release our vindictiveness, we have to identify and overtly express the vindictiveness, the resentments and blame, the grudges we have been nursing since childhood. We can safely and effectively do this by imagining our target in front of us. We direct our attack at the vulnerability of our target. One by one, we express all our vindictive thoughts and feelings to that vulnerable place in the other person and in our self. We lash out at God speaking the thoughts and feelings that have been unspeakable. We need to get it all spoken, all outside of us. By doing this, we break its hold on our life. This experience frees us from blaming in the only way possible, by expelling it from us. It is holy and cleansing. It frees us to experience the richness and abundance of our true emotions, and to live life fully and in the present.

By releasing the self-blame and self-vindictiveness, we open more space within our self to be present to spirit. We forgive our spirit for everything we thought it did and ask for its forgiveness for our lifelong vindictiveness towards it. We recognize and accept our humanity—our innate imperfection as spirit embodied—and experience deep compassion and love for our self. We feel peace within and without.

Having expressed our vindictiveness, we can recognize in a deeper way that mother and father were not to blame; they too came from God. Now we can experience an even deeper form of compassion for them, and forgive them for everything, without exception, that they did to us. We ask them to forgive us for all vindictiveness we have had toward them. We accept them and love them for who they are.

Finally, we can have an experience of God without the barriers of negative love. We recognize God inside of us and outside of us. We can recognize God in each person we meet and in the universe. We experience the vastness that is spirit. We know that God has never rejected us. It's us who have turned away from or rejected God. God is always present to us and within us. When we are present to God, we always find nurturance, joy, peace, strength and love.

Having expressed and released the vindictiveness, we can make freeing, liberating choices for our life. We can choose to give up blaming. We can let go of the past. We can take responsibility for the present, and live our own life.

Blaming tied us to the past and kept us a victim. Being a victim always involves an unwillingness to take responsibility. Our programming of over-responsibility or irresponsibility stood in the way of real responsibility. In negative love we could only react in an unconscious, automatic pattern—prisoners of our programming. Without blame, we regain our ability to respond rather than react. We reclaim the use of choice. We can perceive the vast array of possibilities available to us. We are not victims anymore. We are no longer living our life compulsively and automatically. Our horizons have expanded. We can choose from the abundance. We can do anything we want whether it turns out well or not and we don't have to blame anyone anymore, not even our self. We can be nurturing, supportive and forgiving. Responsibility is the key to our freedom.

Having met this challenge, we feel at peace and joyful. We experience the world differently. The colors are more vibrant, we see the blue of the sky, the petals blowing in the breeze. We are here in the present and it is glorious. We can acknowledge the abundance.

8

Disempowering
Our
Dark Side

*Our patterns fit together, creating a powerful
compulsive internal system that harnesses our
energy and runs our life. This is our dark side.
It robs us of consciousness, and separates
us from our spirit. Through awareness,
commitment and action, we disempower
our dark side, and free our being to
live from our innate positivity.*

When we were conceived, we were in the present moment. Every time we adopted a pattern, a psychic hook was created in us which anchors us to that moment of our childhood. By the time we reached puberty, so many hooks existed that we're lucky we can live in the present at all. Whenever one of our patterns is triggered, we're yanked out of the moment, out of consciousness, into the past, and become that child again. The child within compulsively acts out, in the context of our adult life, the behaviors we learned as a child. Our patterns drive us to re-create the familiar scenarios from childhood—wanting acceptance, expecting rejection and ending up feeling unlovable. We are repeatedly compelled to set our self up to be rejected in numerous different ways. The more conscious we become, the more conscious we are of how often we act unconsciously.

We have felt the power of our compulsive patterns. We have experienced that it's not easy to change, that change takes a long time or doesn't happen at all, that patterns are not easily discarded. Even when we've done the cathartic work we need to do to acknowledge our full being, appreciate and love our self, experience compassion for our parents, our self and others in our life, and choose to take responsibility for our life, we still have the urge to continue in the same old way. We know the power of our compulsivity, the compelling force to stay the same.

Patterns are linked creating vicious cycles

The individual patterns we learned from our parents—the behaviors, moods, attitudes and beliefs—are not isolated and separate. They occur in series. We can easily slip from one pattern into another. It feels completely natural to do so because that's what we've always done. At times, we may feel that the patterns are endless and all-encompassing.

It's valuable to understand how our patterns fit together—that awareness is the beginning of power over them. By mapping out how we move from one pattern to another, we learn that when we are controlled by our patterns, we always end up back where we started. The patterns create a circle, and we're trapped by the compelling energy of the flow—it's really a vicious cycle. In fact, the patterns take on a life of their own and we often feel impotent to stop them. We've all experienced the kind of energy that makes the move from one step to the next seem like the most sensible thing in the world.

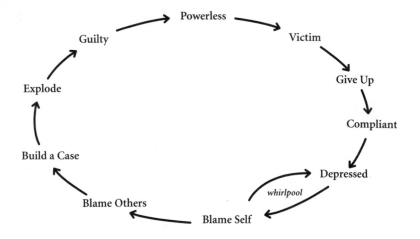

For example, something happens which makes us feel powerless. It seems that the only choice is to go along. We can't expect to have any effect. We are a victim. It appears that we can't get what we want so we give up and become compliant. This leads us into depression. We blame our self for being so weak, for being a victim. This makes us more depressed and more self-blaming, and more depressed. We become stuck in a whirlpool of depression and self-blame for days or even longer. It's an awful place to be. Finally we can't take it anymore. We look outside our self for someone else to blame. We build a case against them until the rage and anger explodes and gives us a sense of power. Then we feel wrong and bad and guilty. And we move back into powerless again, poised to start all over again.

We've been doing it for our whole life. It feels familiar. The pathways are worn and smooth, and we sail easily from one pattern to another. We can go all around a cycle and be oblivious to the fact that we touched more than one or two places, or even that we have been in the cycle at all. Many of us have lived most of our life in one cycle or another. We defend the feelings, thoughts and actions as if they are us.

Each of us has our own way of moving through our unique set of patterns, our own trigger points, and many ways of getting stuck. If we draw a lot of our vicious cycles, we can see how they fit together at numerous points—one cycle interconnects with various others creating a powerful inner web of compulsivity. When we perceive our patterns together, interwoven into interconnecting cycles of negativity—not just individually—we can begin to understand the extent of their power.

Structure harnesses our energy

Whenever things are organized into a system, there is always more energy, strength and power than when the same items exist individually or alone. Structure makes systems energy-efficient. The structure of our inner web harnesses our energy, and the system takes on a life of its own. This maze of compulsivity has tremendous magnetic energy to draw us into it and keep us living as though the patterns are the truth. We know this because we've all felt the power of our compulsive behavior.

We have the best of intentions, we know that is in our best interest to take care of our self and be loving and nurturing to our self. We may even make the decision to act on our intentions and take care of our self. Yet, we do something to undermine that decision: we don't follow through or we do something directly harmful to us. And then we ask our self, "Why did I do that?"

At times we may have felt like we are two people. One is open, curious, eager to learn and grow, knowledgeable, caring and giving. And the other one is a saboteur using justification, arguments, judgments and "rational lies" to reject the best part of us, and to reject others in our life who might come too close or care too much. Sometimes we are clearly aware that what we want to do is absolutely the wrong thing to do, and yet we go ahead and do it anyway.

The Dark Side controls us like a robot

Some of us have actually felt that there is a monster living inside of us whose only drive is to survive—it doesn't care about our well-being. And there is this part in all of us. It's the embodiment of all of our negative love patterns interacting and controlling us automatically and compulsively. It has no intentions. It knows only compulsion. It is an auto-pilot that was set in our childhood. It turns us into a robot under its programmed command. We call this energy-packed system, this totality of all our negative love patterns, the dark side.

Our dark side has controlled us throughout our life. It sends the messages in our head, the messages that come when we're most vulnerable. "Nothing you do will have any effect. You can't change that easily. You're incompetent. You don't need anyone else. You're bad. Life's a struggle. Don't expect much. This is the way you really are. You don't deserve—love, money, success. You're stupid. God doesn't exist. You're going to fail. I know it all. Be responsible. Work like crazy. Money is the key to happiness. Women are weak. This can't last. You're ugly. Men are dangerous. Sex isn't important, or it's all important. Blacks/Whites/Asians aren't trustworthy. Fun is all that matters. The end justifies the means."

The traumas in our life have been created by our dark side, this composite of all of our compulsivity. The losses and abuse we've endured and created. The relationships we've destroyed. The pain we've inflicted on others and on our self, the self-destructive acts, the opportunities we've missed.

For example, we drink too much and insist on driving and have an accident in our car, which injures us and others. This is our dark side. Or we angrily yell at our children and threaten them because they are making too much noise. And we know we should have spoken to them differently, that it really is just youthful exuberance. But we justify our action because we are tired and they need to learn. This is our dark side. Or our lover enthusiastically compliments another person's achievement and we feel jealous even though we feel the compliments are deserved. We fight with our beloved even though we know we are wrong to do so. Then later we want to apologize for being so silly, but we don't. Instead we rationalize that as a result of what we said, next time our beloved will be more careful about paying attention to another. This is our dark side. Or we are in recovery and working hard to change our life, and some old friends drop by and start smoking pot and we don't say anything because we don't want to make them feel bad. And then, of course, they offer some to us and we refuse it and they tease us, and we take some and start smoking. This is our dark side. Or we feel mistreated at work. We come home annoyed. We get into an argument with our wife, blame her for triggering the anger. And when she defends herself, we beat her up. This is our dark side.

Each of us come from a family system that is transmitted from our parents' dark side to ours. Our dark side is programmed to be in control forever. Our dark side contains all the beliefs that limit our life. It includes the values that compel us to experience others as superior or inferior to us but never equal, our prejudices that people are not good because they are a certain nationality, ethnic heritage, color, because they have a certain sexual or religious preference, because they are rich or poor, because they are different from us.

Our collective dark sides
are reflected in the world

The world is a macrosystem of families which reflects and magnifies our individual dark sides collectively. Each of us operates in the world with our own set of negative love patterns, our own dark side, and we find and recreate our familial system in society.

Look at our world. Competition is everywhere, like siblings fighting to be the best, stealing from one another, manipulating, lying with one feeling superior and another inferior, ignoring each other. There can be no equality. Our politicians in government cannot do what's needed to right the injustices because they are addicted to power. Some of us have too much and others have nothing. Homeless people die without food or clothes and we feel that this is not our responsibility. We blame others. The poor blame the rich and the rich blame the poor. No one takes responsibility. Our prejudices are institutionalized. Wars are ever present. We battle over religious differences, which God exists or is better. Material possessions, money, status, prestige, power and social position drive us to step upon each other. We live in fear of losing our possessions or envious of others with more. We destroy our environment which supports our very life, cutting down the forests, polluting the land, air and water, decreasing the quality of our life. We have lost our idealism, our hope for a better world. This is our collective dark side. What we have inside of us is what we put out into the world.

Just as our negative love patterns are not us, so the energy system that is the dark side is a parasite on us. It lives on our intellect and uses our intellect's abilities to play out its patterns. It's the part that holds onto addictions, the part that holds on to all our automatic behavior, moods, attitudes and beliefs. It knows nothing but compulsivity. It is driven to recreate the past in order to survive. When we abdicate our responsibility, the dark side gains control of our life. We become a victim of our negative programming. Whenever we are in one of our compulsive patterns, our dark side is in charge and it is using our energy and depleting our resources. The longer this continues, the stronger our dark side grows.

The dark side can never be re-educated. It is rigid and inflexible. It can not compromise or collaborate. Our dark side is a robot that could only be programmed during our childhood. Our childhood is over even if our child lives on.

Disempowering our dark side requires commitment and action

We cannot kill our dark side. As humans we are by definition imperfect, and our imperfections are the patterns of which the dark side is composed. We can diminish our dark side through disconnecting from the specific negative patterns and transforming them into positive alternatives. But since we can never be perfect, our dark side will never completely disappear.

We need to disempower our dark side so it doesn't control us. The system needs to be inactivated. This involves awareness, commitment and action.

First, we identify specifically how our life has been driven by the compulsivity of our dark side. We identify its programmed messages, its patterns. We watch the way we live unconsciously, observe the compulsivity for what it actually does in our life. We recognize how we feel when we are acting from that compulsivity, what it does to us, what it does to the people we love and others in our life. We get a clear picture of what our dark side has created in our life—the loss, alienation, pain and suffering.

Then, we imagine our dark side as a monster. It certainly has had monstrous effects on our life. Some of us have seen its face already in our nightmares. We've felt our self to be two people. Our intellect has two heads in direct opposition to one another. They represent the choice between compulsivity and free will so there can be no effective truce.

Next, we recognize that the spirit in us and beyond us is always stronger than the power of the dark side. Our dark side always separates us from the light and makes us believe that we must *do* something to be spirit. When the dark side controls us, we lose touch with our essence. We *are* spirit, and we must invoke our spirit to take our power back. Our spirit is not a tyrant, or dictator. The light, the spirit, never takes us over as the dark side does. We must choose light. We must recognize the light within us and call it forth. This requires awareness and commitment.

Having made the choice, we speak our commitment to disempower and dismantle our dark side, and claim control of our own life. We speak out loud. In the speaking, we dis-identify our authentic being from the compulsive patterns and claim our wholeness, our goodness, our inner wisdom, our power and energy, and our love. As we speak, we hear hidden, unknown truths come from deep inside us. We empower our positive intellect and free our emotional child, spirit and body to live authentically. We vow to disempower and further dismantle our dark side when it reappears. We envoke the power of commitment.

When we disempower our dark side and claim our own energy, we are present to our whole being. We feel grounded, energetic and confident. We know who we are, and we can live authentically. We are in touch with our inner wisdom and joy. We take responsibility for our life and our actions. We recognize and accept our humanity, our innate imperfection. We recognize that we will never be free of the dark side, but we can increase our awareness, and we know how to take our energy back when the dark side grabs control. We know God in us and in every person. We grasp the importance of understanding and forgiveness, starting with us. We relate with love and compassion. Our relationships change. We make decisions that nurture us, others and the environment.

9

Reclaiming
Our Joy

*Our changes broaden our perspective, and
new truths become visible. We can reclaim
the childlike spontaneity, playfulness and joy
which is us. We are able to perceive and
validate the positive attitudes and skills
learned from and nurtured by our parents.
This restores balance to our lives.*

W e were conceived as joyous beings full of love and curiosity. Our essence is love. Our nature is spontaneous, present to the moment and the abundance of the choices available. We were born playful and bubbling with laughter. Bliss was a daily experience. We've lost touch with this.

In our childhood, as a result of negative love, we learned to focus on what was wrong in our life, and tried to correct our self. We spent little or no time validating the wonderful things about our self—our intelligence, curiosity, sense of adventure, playfulness, courage, willingness to risk, openness, perseverance, generosity, laughter, kindness and joy. As a result we grew up with a negative view of our self, of others and of the world.

Our negative scanner

We are practiced at discerning what's wrong. We were trained to be like this. We have an internal negative scanner that evaluates us, the situation and others. It quickly hones in on the negative, examines it, and in doing so expands it. Then our scanner moves on to another negative and creates the same expansion, until it has highlighted each and every deficit. In the process it often skips right over what's good in us, in others and in the world, as if these are unremarkable.

When we think about negative things, most of us can spend a great amount of time and energy describing all the details and examining an event from every possible perspective. We talk about what we feel, how others feel, what each of us was thinking, our intentions, how we can possibly change this situation, how we've done things in the past, and they didn't work. We often have tremendous patience for negativity because we have learned as a child to expect it. We can easily enter into that negative space with our self, with family and friends, with co-workers, even with casual acquaintances.

Negativity is acceptable. The news in papers, magazines and television focuses on the negative events of the world. They too give great detail and display photographs so it's indelibly printed on our mind. The beliefs, "life is a struggle," "the world is a dangerous place," and "change is difficult," play out in our everyday life.

Reaction to feedback from others

Think about when we are honestly complimented. A friend says we look beautiful today, our eyes have a special sparkle and loveliness. Or our boss says that the project we just finished is fabulous, reflecting our creativity and dedication. We often feel uncomfortable, embarrassed, undeserving. Perhaps we blush and tell them to stop, while inside we are criticizing them or wondering what they thought of us before, or when they are going to find us out.

But if this same person comes to us with constructive criticism, we may want all the details, even if we resent having them pointed out, and defend our self vigorously. We can talk on and on. We feel comfortable focusing on our deficiencies. Daily we criticize our self, making lists of how we need to change.

How do we speak of positive qualities, behaviors, events—our own, or others? Do we even notice? Many of us find it difficult or impossible to give compliments which reflect our true admiration and respect for others, or for our self. We may think of them, but rarely put them into words. We often feel just as uneasy giving compliments as we do receiving them. Do we make a point of regularly validating the talents, abilities, strengths and achievements of our children and spouse? Or do we criticize them constantly with the intention of making them into better people?

Play and celebrations in childhood

Remember the times in our childhood when we were having fun, alone or with others. We were expressing our playfulness, our enthusiasm and our spontaneity totally involved in the joy of the moment. Were we made to stop or criticized for making too much noise? At times there was music, and we moved around the room with abandon enjoying the sensation of our bodies moving in space. Did our parents say, "Not like that, let me show you how to dance." And now we are self-conscious about our body, about dancing, about our sensuality. Remember the times we were lost in the joy of playing, and our parents told us that's enough playing or that's enough laughing. They made us believe there's a time limit on fun and laughter, on abandon. We mustn't have too much. Even when we went to our parents to express our love, there may have been admonishments. They may have asked, "What do you want? Why are you so loving today?" Or they were too busy to receive it.

In our childhood there were times of celebration: our birthdays, Christmas, Hanukkah, New Year, Easter, the 4th of July. Were they truly happy, joyful occasions? Were we celebrated on our birthday as the center of attention, surrounded by our friends and family, doing what we wanted to do, and receiving gifts that reflected love and caring? Or was it a time for our parents to throw a party for their friends? Did they get frustrated with all the work, annoyed with the noise? Did they drink too much, getting drunk and angry? Did they pay someone to create a party for us so they wouldn't have to be bothered? Did they shower us with gifts, but not their presence and attention? Was our birthday minimized or ignored? How did our parents relate to their own birthdays? As an adult, how do we deal with our birthday? Do we hide and ignore it, feeling depressed? Do we even resent it if someone who loves us wants to celebrate it? Do we demand extravagant celebrations just so we can be the center of attention? Are our celebrations empty? Do we always feel disappointed? Do we forget the birthdays of others, and create disappointments in our relationships?

Look at how Christmas, Hanukkah and New Year were in our childhood. Was it a frenzy of preparation and gift-buying with worry about time and money, so there was no space for giving and receiving of love, attention, companionship? Did our parents encourage us to write a list of gifts we wanted, raising our expectations, and then give us none of them or only one, so now we don't expect to get what we want in life? Or did they give us everything so now we feel disappointed if we don't get everything we want? Were we made to feel a part of our family and the community? Was the celebration focused on the adults and were we pushed out of the way? Did it culminate in parties where everyone ate too much and drank too much? Was the meaning of the holidays lost because it was only obligatory activities, gifts and boring parties? How do we celebrate and enjoy the holidays now? What are our expectations? At New Year do we recognize and validate the wonderful things we have accomplished in the last year, or do we focus only on what we don't have? We make resolutions to change, improve our relationships, stop addictions, and then quickly lose our will or even our memory of what we decided.

Play in adulthood

We learned from our parents what it is to be an adult. We probably learned that adulthood is serious, tense, responsibility and achievement oriented. There's little time for fun. Look at the way we have fun in our adult life. Our play is often structured into competition with someone winning and others losing. We always have to achieve something— catch a fish, build a trellis, close a business deal on the golf course. Is our work the way we have fun? How much of what we call fun is socializing to assuage our loneliness? Do we use alcohol or drugs to escape from our self and call it fun? Do we use sarcasm as our form of humor, putting someone down, our self or others?

Our essence is playful and positive

In reality, our authentic being is positive, and only the false acquired self, our dark side, is negative. The negativity is like a monkey that is always busy, and as a result has held our attention for most of our life, while the much more substantial positivity is quietly waiting in a hammock. Often when we focus on our negativity, we are simply feeding it our energy, and the negativity appears to grow larger. We may have the false belief that simply focusing on our faults will make them eventually dissipate. We may have also tried to deny and repress any negativity, acting falsely positive, putting on a happy face in an attempt to give our self and others what we want.

On this journey we learn to identify the parental patterns that compelled and sabotaged our life, then to step back from them, disown them and push them out of our life. In accomplishing this, we gain a broader perspective. We can put our energy into awakening our positivity, which is always stronger than the negative. We can reclaim our inner core of positivity and joy.

Having cleared out the negative past, we are often amazed at how many positive memories come flooding back. They may appear as simple events, but these moments have enriched and colored our lives. We remember positive experiences of childhood, happy times filled with joy and laughter and wonderful feelings. It's important to claim each one in detail. We can look inside our self and recognize the many positive qualities we have. We identify the goodness that is in our adult lives because of these qualities. One by one we can acknowledge how we learned each of these from our parents in our childhood. We learned positive things from our parents and we need to become conscious of them. We do this to give energy to our positivity, to claim these wonderful qualities that we never need to change.

There are many examples. They taught us to walk and speak. They cared for our body. They said, "You are beautiful." They validated our curiosity. They helped us with our homework. They complimented the drawings we made. They played with us, sang for us. They read books to us, and told us stories. They entered into our child's world. They gave us an unexpected gift. They created celebrations. They taught us how to cook and take care of the house, how to build things. They prayed with us and taught us about the goodness of God. They taught us to ride a bike, and encouraged us, saying over and over, "You can do it," and we could and we were so proud and happy. Remember the times they spent with us that were tranquil and we felt protected.

We learned how to care for our body, giving it food and rest, keeping it clean and well-clothed, caring for it in illness. We learned to read and write, to appreciate books, ideas and imagination. We learned how to relate to people in a respectful manner. We learned to marvel at nature and enjoy the colors of flowers, the beauty of dew on the leaves, a spider's web, the wonder of growth from a little seed into a strong plant. We learned to build things seeing the relationship between structure, function and beauty. We learned the joy of shared laughter and warm nurturing humor. We learned to be affectionate. We learned the pleasure of moving our body in dance, exercise and sports, enjoying the pleasures of nature. They brought us to the joy of music, listening to it, dancing with it, creating it and playing with it. They taught us to love animals, caring for them and playing with them. We learned responsibility and commitment. We learned how to overcome adversity. They taught us about work and money. We learned how to manage in the world.

The time we spend remembering and describing each of these experiences brings joy to our heart. We know that our childhood holds much to be proud of. We don't have to change these positive traits. We only need to recognize them and validate them. Our parents did so much for us despite their programming, and because of this, in our adulthood we do the same for our self, our children and others in our life. We are thankful for how their efforts and their spirits have enriched our lives.

We can't change our childhood, but we can change our view of it. In negative love we are stuck in one perspective. We see the negative and repress the positive, and blame our parents. Or we see the only positive and repress the negative, and blame our self for our life. It isn't all one way or the other. In recognizing both the negativity that resulted from negative love and the positivity which prevails despite the programming, we gain a balanced perspective of our life and of our parents.

Recycling the negative into positive alternatives

When we reach this point in the journey, we are ready to transform our negative compulsive patterns into positive alternatives. We envision the negative pattern, from which we have already disconnected, occurring in an actual recent situation. We then visualize moving the pattern outside our being and de-energizing it. Then we tap into our inner wisdom by asking our spirit to show us a positive alternative that is appropriate for us. We call this *recycling*. As we recycle each of our negative patterns one by one, the details of a new self-image emerge, and we feel our energy shift. Now when faced with a particular situation, instead of the old pattern automatically playing out, we find our self consciously choosing a new positive alternative which works much more effectively. In fact, we find the recycled patterns diminishing or even disappearing from our life without effort.

Moving through the various stages of this journey, our emotional child speaks its truth and reclaims its full range of feelings and expressiveness. Our intellect gains understanding, acknowledging the sources of the goodness in its life. They have made a truce with each other to work together and learn from each other and to be present to our body.

Play as a spontaneous expression of self

Finally our child can be the teacher of the intellect and teach it to express joyfulness in play. Our intellect gives itself permission to learn to play like a child with no purpose and no design. Our essence is joyous and spontaneous. We experience play as a spontaneous expression of self that makes us feel good about being alive, that renews and relaxes us. Positive play is its own goal. It doesn't have to accomplish anything. It just is. Laughter actually changes our body chemistry and changes our mood. This is reclaiming the repressed childlike part of us.

As well as playing alone, it's vital to play with a group, interacting with exuberance, laughter and joy—being in the present moment with each other. This is especially true if we have been loners in life. Playfulness opens us to possibility and yields healing and balance. This play experience is just as important as any we have described throughout this journey, but it is one that we may feel is extraneous and frivolous. Those of us who feel that way are the ones who need it the most.

It's important to change our relationship to celebrations in our life—our own birthdays as well as others, holidays, and other special occasions. We approach them with the joyous simplicity and importance of a child, really connecting with our loved one, creating experiences that bring out the wonderful childlike joy in all who participate.

When we can recognize and enjoy the positivity of our self and others, we can develop a scanner that is ever aware of the positivity in life. We will find that when we focus on our positivity without judgment, appreciating and validating it, the negative naturally loses energy and becomes smaller. In this way we nurture the positive in our self, in our relationships and in the world.

The journey has taken us through all the consequences of the negativity in our life to free our self from it. We have gone through all the positivity to be free of value judgments about what's negative and what's positive. Good and bad are relative. What's good for us, may be bad for another. Work and play are both needed for a balanced harmonious life. The journey enables us to experience things as they are. We can be truly thankful to our parents for the many wonderful things that they did for us. We can feel joy inside of our self, in others and in nature. We have reclaimed our bliss.

10

Achieving Integration

The necessity of each of our four aspects—spirit, emotions, intellect and body—can now be recognized as essential for life. Our emotional child matures, and all aspects integrate as equal adult partners committed to collaboration and teamwork. We love our whole being the way we have always wanted to be loved, and, finally, can receive love from others and love unconditionally.

During this journey, we rediscover the essential value of each of our four aspects. We see their individual strengths. We recognize that each is vital to our being.

Our inner emotional child has worked diligently. With great courage our child disconnected from our negative past, and now experiences feelings in the moment. We can recognize the difference between the reactivity of a compulsive pattern and the responsiveness of a feeling. We have regained our ability to allow our feelings to flow, welcoming them all as valuable reflections of our reality without judgment. Now our child is ready and eager to grow up and become an emotional adult, leaving behind our reactivity and defensiveness, and taking into adulthood our wonderful childlike qualities—our joy, enthusiasm, curiosity and spontaneity.

Our adult intellect has been able to remove the blindfold of negative love. It understands how it came to be programmed through our emotional child. Putting aside intellectual defenses, we have opened our self to seeing the truth, examined our preconceived values, thoughts and beliefs, and we can discern what is real. We have grown and learned and become re-educated.

Our emotional child and adult intellect have confronted each other and have committed to working together. Now our child can listen to our intellect, and our intellect can listen to our child and together make wise decisions for our life.

Our spirit has been re-discovered experientially. We can recognize the existence of this precious part of our being. We know our spirit is the voice of truth and wisdom inside us. It is the source of our vision and creativity. It is love. Our spirit connects us to the universe and to the abundance. We have created space for spirit to express itself and be heard. We can commit to working with our spirit, and living from our positivity.

Our physical body has been released from the constrictions of the past. It is recognized by our child and intellect as a vital and informative part of us. It is lighter, more agile and more expressive. There is a sparkle in our eyes and an aliveness in our face. We have more energy.

All four aspects are prepared to come together and form a new harmonious partnership based on equality, collaboration and love. We are ready to integrate all parts of our being.

Integration—an inner marriage

We visualize our self in the security of our sanctuary surrounded by light. The spirits of our parents, grandparents, siblings, spouse or lover, children and other important people in our lives are present as witnesses.

We experience our emotional child being reborn as a positive child freed from negative programming. Our spirit and intellect fill our newly reborn child with love, and validate it for who it really is. Nurtured by this unconditional love and acceptance, we experience our emotional child growing up and maturing into a wonderfully positive, loving, adult emotional self, who takes its rightful place next to our adult intellect as its equal.

Our positive intellect and adult emotional self accept and understand each other just as they are. They experience and express compassion, forgiveness and love for each other. As equal loving adults, they commit themselves to working together as equal partners throughout this lifetime. They agree to be truthful, open, supportive and nurturing, and to help each other continue to learn and grow.

In the presence of the Light of the Universe, the three aspects of our mind—emotions, intellect, and spirit—feel the loving energy of the light flowing from one aspect to another, intermingling the energies. Each aspect becomes more the other. The light disperses the darkness of residual negativity. Each aspect promises to understand, accept and love the others. The three are united by the light in an equal partnership, an inner marriage. This integration of the three aspects of our mind enables us to experience a deeper form of communion with the light than we have had before.

Forgiveness and love bring freedom

Now as one united mind, our three aspects approach our parents. We express our understanding of what they did without any blame. We express our compassion, acceptance and love for each of them. We give and receive forgiveness. We look into our mother's and father's eyes with the recognition that they are not their patterns. We know that they were driven by their programmed child inside them to do what they did to us. Now we understand. We see their beautiful light essence within and have respect for them as individuals. Now we really love them.

We can look into the eyes of our adult mother, and say from our heart, "I love you, Mother." We can look into our father's eyes, and say from our heart, "I love you, Father." We are able to give selflessly without expecting anything in return. We can give to them because we truly love our self. We are in touch with the abundance of love within us. We don't need to look to our parents and depend on them for love or anything else anymore.

We envision the twisted cords of negative love running from our grandparents to our parents and then to us, the ties that have bound us together in negativity from generation to generation. We rip the cords out of our self. We don't need to be negatively attached anymore. We have learned how to transform the negativity in our life. We don't need to go through life relating to others as if they are our mother and father. Now we can relate with our parents, and others in our life, from our essence to theirs.

From this perspective, we recognize how many negative things we have done in our life without knowing what we were doing, driven by our compelling patterns. We free our self and others from the negativity of the past. We clean the slate so we can start to live our life from this moment in a new way.

We can communicate with each of the important people in our life—our grandparents, siblings, children, lovers, ex-lovers, friends and co-workers. We ask them for forgiveness for every wrong that we did to them, consciously or unconsciously. We can forgive all the people who ever did hurtful things to us, even the people we never liked. Resentment and guilt make us a prisoner, a victim. We are determined to free our being, and to free these people too. We free all of us from guilt and obligation by forgiving. Then we become ready once more to start living life from our essence.

Integrating our body

Finally we turn our attention to the home where our mind lives, our physical body. We make the commitment to care for our body with respect, acceptance, pleasure and love. We commit to listening to our body and responding to its messages. We promise to nurture it and treasure it as the temple of our spirit. Our body is vital for the experience and expression of feelings, thoughts and spirit. Through it we express our love and caring. Through our sexuality we express all aspects of our self—our thoughts, feelings, spirituality and sensuality—and feel at one with our self and with another. Our body welcomes our newly positive mind into it. Together all four aspects experience unity as an integrated, harmonious quadrinity—the inner marriage is now complete.

At our conception God blessed each of us with free will. This ability to choose conferred dignity on us and instilled responsibility in us for our self, others and the world. Negative love distorts this gift. Achieving integration restores harmony and balance in our being. As integrated beings we can choose to live from our free will because we know who we are, what we are doing, what we can do and what we want to do. We have stepped outside of our patterns. We know we are responsible for everything in our life. Our choices expand to encompass the abundance of reality.

We find what we have been looking for, and it is us. We are love and we are loving. We love our self the way we have always wanted to be loved. In fact, the only person who can love us this way is our self. When we love our self in this way, we feel full of love. We are connected to the abundance and know it is limitless. We can share our unconditional love with others in our life. We do not need anything in return. We can live life in peace and love. We can live each day in the present as if the present is the only day we have. We live life as an adventure open to the possibilities.

The quality of our relationships change

When we see our mother and father in person, we see the emotional child inside of them, and we know that their child didn't receive the love it yearned for. We can give love to them without asking for anything in return. We accept them just the way they are and see their spirit within.

We can recognize that our siblings were victims of negative love just like we were, and give them compassion and love. We feel deeper respect and love for our spouse or lover, more curiosity about who they really are and we experience more understanding and acceptance, even if we are uncertain of our relationship with them. We know what intimacy is, and we can integrate sexuality and love.

We care for our children in a different way, seeing them as separate from us. We can be more authentic with them and present to them. We recognize their talents and give them validation and direction. We see the patterns that they learned from us and have compassion for them. We don't blame them or our self. We know we all did the best we could.

We are a better friend, able to give and receive in the relationship and share with each other. We work with greater satisfaction and balance and use our money well. We know that this body is the only one we have for this lifetime and learn to treasure it. We transform our relationship to sickness and even find healing.

We can understand, through our limited individual history, the history of all humanity because negative love drives us all. Everyone has a reason for being the way they are. We realize that we are not our patterns or problems and others are not their patterns or problems either. We know that all of us are striving for love and integration, and we feel humble in our achievement.

We do not feed energy to the negativities in our self, in others, or in the world. We can live from our spirit and our positivity. We are in control of our life now. We choose our path and we choose our response to whatever comes our way.

Negative love is compelling and its consequences are diverse and complex. We need to stay awake all our life. Our challenge is to be present in the moment—each moment—and take our responsibility seriously. We are human—spirit embodied—and we will never be perfect. Recognizing this, we know that there's always more to learn. Life is change and we have inner guidance and wisdom. We continue to grow all the time. As we grow and expand in our lives, we recognize other patterns that limit us and we can disconnect from them and recycle them to reach greater presence and awareness. We can feel proud of our accomplishments. We can recognize how much real quality we can bring into our life, how much love we can give to our self and others, and how much positive energy we can contribute to the world.

Accomplishing Growth

W e have traced a powerful inner journey into love. It is a hero's journey to wholeness, to authenticity and integration. Each step has its own logic and goal. Each step is critical for achieving the whole. It's intense, focused and directed. It's a journey which culminates in integration, and yet never ends.

As imperfect human beings, we cannot maintain the integration at every moment. We lose it each time we are triggered into a negative pattern. Patterns yank us back to our childhood. Then we must use our free will to become conscious and choose to act to bring our self back into integration. The more patterns we identify and disconnect from, the fewer triggers exist that take us back to childhood, and the more time we can spend connected and present to our self and others. As we disconnect from specific patterns, we remove the filters that allow other patterns finally to be seen. So the journey continues.

We have written as simply and clearly as we could about the ten steps on this transforming journey that yield profound and lasting changes in each of us who have traveled this way.

Reading about this journey brings awareness and intellectual understanding. It enlivens our hope for our life. It can move us to commit to change. But only by fully experiencing the journey for our self, identifying and expressing our feelings, accomplishing the catharsis required by each step, can we know the abundance of the goal. This journey is truly experiential education.

We want to reach the destination. We want to love our

self. And we may feel overwhelmed and discouraged by the apparent effort involved. It is an intense journey that requires courage, commitment and determination.

Thousands of people have successfully faced these challenges in countries around the world. People have been benefiting from this journey for almost a third of a century. Many thousands of people have changed their lives, and the dynamic of their families—in some cases, whole families including grandparents, parents, spouses and children. This path is about finding love and peace within our being, in our family and in the world.

The journey into love is expansive work which creates space inside of us and connects us with our inner wisdom. It releases our creativity and opens us to possibilities we had no idea existed. We establish intimacy with our self—the ability to know our self and be who we really are. And we learn how to create intimacy with others in our life through sharing our realities and our love.

The journey starts with the first challenge—awareness. You have begun.

Journey Into Love:
Ten Steps to Wholeness

1 Moving into Awareness
The journey into love begins with understanding how we lost sight of our essence, our spirit, our source of love. In order to survive in childhood we took on a false self comprised of compulsive patterns which are not us, but define, control and limit us. Awareness that these patterns are not us, brings us hope that we can change.

2 Committing to Change
Our desire to change our self and our life arises from our dissatisfaction with what is, regardless of how successful and fulfilled our life appears to be. Hope that change is possible, along with recognition of the specifics of what's wrong with our life, moves us to commit to change. Commitment energizes the change process and enables it to flow.

3 Acknowledging Our Essence
Compulsive patterns disrupt our connection with our essence which is love. Re-experiencing and acknowledging that our spiritual essence is love reveals our patterns as separate from us and opens us to our inner wisdom. We can envision living from our truth. We are empowered to proceed from strength rather than weakness.

4 Getting the Anger Out
To escape the hurt, fear and abandonment we felt as a child, we got angry. Suppressed and denied, that anger from our childhood surfaces today as resentment, depression, illness and violence. By focusing our anger's expression at the source of the pain, we move the parents of our childhood outside of us, establish clear boundaries and claim our self.

5 Finding Forgiveness and Compassion
Having released our anger, the path takes us into the reality of our parents' childhoods. Deep emotional understanding of their lives brings forgiveness, and compassion for the child that lives in each of them. In giving them unconditional love, we can finally experience compassionate forgiveness and love for our self.

6 Ending the Battle Within

Freed from negative attachment to our parents, we face the war within. The internal battle between child and intellect has stressed our body and obscured our essence. Expressing the grievances makes space for a truce, an agreement to work together in partnership and harmony, and create inner peace.

7 Moving Beyond Blame

Finally we see that blaming our self and others keeps us negatively attached to the past, and limits us to fantasizing a better future. We keep missing the moment. Moving beyond the compulsive blaming and desire for revenge restores our ability to live in the present with responsiveness and choice.

8 Disempowering Our Dark Side

Our patterns fit together, creating a powerful compulsive internal system that harnesses our energy and runs our life. This is our dark side. It robs us of consciousness, and separates us from our spirit. Through awareness, commitment and action, we can disempower our dark side, and free our being to live from our innate positivity.

9 Reclaiming Our Joy

Our changes broaden our perspective, and new truths become visible. We can reclaim the childlike spontaneity, playfulness and joy which is us. We are able to perceive and validate the positive attitudes and skills learned from and nurtured by our parents. This restores balance to our lives.

10 Achieving Integration

The necessity of each of our four aspects—spirit, emotions, intellect and body—can now be recognized as essential for life. Our emotional child matures, and all aspects integrate as equal adult partners committed to collaboration and teamwork. We love our whole being the way we have always wanted to be loved, and, finally, can receive love from others and love unconditionally.

Appendix

Hoffman Quadrinity Process®

The basis for the journey that we have described is a process created by Bob Hoffman in 1967 in the United States, and brought to Brazil in 1974. Initially Hoffman worked with individuals one-to-one. Then in 1972, at the suggestion of the well-known psychiatrist and author, Claudio Naranjo, Hoffman developed the more powerful group sessions using a 13-week format. The students met with the group weekly for three to five hours, had one-to-one sessions with their assigned teacher, and did individual assignments on their own. In 1985 Hoffman re-designed the work into the current seven-day residential program which includes all the elements of the original format and more. This new format increases the intensity and continuity of the process, avoiding the multiple transitions between the carthartic experiences and normal life. In addition, it provides the continuous presence, support and guidance of the highly trained and skilled teaching staff. In this safe space with supportive teachers and focused inward for seven days, students are able to go very deep and accomplish tremendous growth.

The seven-day residential format has also made the work more accessible to people throughout the world. As a result, it is now offered in authorized centers in various places across the United States, and in many countries in the world including Argentina, Australia, Brazil, Canada, France, Germany, Ireland, Italy, South Africa, Spain, Switzerland and United Kingdom under the official name: Hoffman Quadrinity Process®.

For more information, please contact one of the following centers:

Process taught in English:
Hoffman Centre - Australia
230 Toorak Road, Suite 3 (First Floor)
South Yarra, Victoria 3141 Australia
61-3-9826-2133 phone   61-3-9826-2144 fax
website: quadrinity.com.au

Hoffman Institute - Canada
109 Edgehill Drive
Kitchener, Ontario
N2P 2C8 Canada
519-650-1755 phone 519-650-5590 fax
website: www.hoffmaninstitute.ca

Hoffman Institute - Ireland
353-1-820-4477 phone
website: hoffmanireland.com

Hoffman Institute - Singapore
PO Box 734 Tanglin Post Office
Singapore 912425
65-254-3851 phone   65-254-9489
website: www.quadrinity.com.au

Hoffman Institute - United Kingdom
The Old Post House
Burpham, Arundel
BN18 9RH United Kingdom
44-1903-88-9990 phone   44-1903-88-9991 fax
website: www.hoffmaninstitute.co.uk

Hoffman Institute - USA
1299 Fourth Street Suite 304
San Rafael, CA 94901
800/506-5253 phone   415/485-5539 fax
website: www.hoffmaninstitute.org

Process taught in language other than English:
Hoffman Institute - Argentina
Santa Fé 3796, 2f A
Ciudad de Buenos Aires, Argentina
5411-4833-2872 phone   5411-4833-2567 fax
website: www.quadrinidad.com.br

Centro Hoffman da Quadrinidade - Brasil
Rua Pio XI no 1231
Sao Paulo, SP, Brasil
CEP 05060-001
55 (11) 3832-3050 or 55 (11) 3832-4497 phone/fax
website: www.centrohoffman.com.br

Institut Hoffman - France
Jaegerhaeusleweg 32
D-79104 Freiburg, Germany
0049-761-55-2966 phone
0049-761-56843 fax
website: www.institut-hoffman.com

Hoffman Institute - Germany
Postfach 304004
10725 Berlin, Germany
49-30-217-6613 phone
49-30-217-7719 fax
website: www.quadrinity.de

Hoffman Institute - Germany
Linienstrasse 70
D-40227 Düsseldorf, Germany
49-(0)700-2525-2100 phone
49-(0)700-2525-2101 fax
website: www.hoffman-quadrinity-institut.de

Hoffman Institute - Italia
Via Bramante, 39
20154 Milano, Italy
39-02-3493-8382 phone
39-02-3491-266 fax
website: www.quadrinity.it

Hoffman Institute - Spain
San Francisco 1-3 01001 Vitoria, Spain
34-945-27-1733 phone/fax

Hoffman Institute - Switzerland
IAK Institut für Angewandte
Kurzzeittherapie GmbH
St. Galler Strasse 1
9470 Buchs SG, Switzerland
41-81-740-0284 phone
41-81-740-0285 fax
website: www.iak-quadrinity.ch

Hoffman Institute International
3100 White Sulphur Springs Road
St. Helena, CA 94574
707-968-0810 phone/fax
website: www.quadrinity.com

About the Authors

Kani Comstock is a teacher of the Hoffman Quadrinity Process, was director of the Hoffman Institute worldwide and in the United States for many years, and has been working with the Process since 1986. She lives in southern Oregon.

Marisa Thame was a psychotherapist, founder and director of the Hoffman Institute for Brazil and Latin America, a director of Hoffman Institute International 1997-2002, and a teacher of the Hoffman Quadrinity Process for over 20 years. She lived in Sao Paulo, Brazil.